The
Little Green Book
of
ECO-FASCISM

The
Little Green Book
— of —
ECO-FASCISM

The Left's Plan to Frighten Your Kids, Drive Up Energy Costs, and Hike Your Taxes!

JAMES DELINGPOLE

REGNERY
Publishing, Inc.
An Eagle Publishing Company • Washington, DC

Cataloging-in-Publication data on file with the Library of Congress

ISBN 978-1-62157-161-2

Published in the United States by
Regnery Publishing, Inc.
One Massachusetts Avenue NW
Washington, DC 20001
www.Regnery.com

Manufactured in the United States of America

10 9 8 7 6 5 4 3 2 1

Books are available in quantity for promotional or premium use. Write to Director of Special Sales, Regnery Publishing, Inc., One Massachusetts Avenue NW, Washington, DC 20001, for information on discounts and terms, or call (202) 216-0600.

Distributed to the trade by
Perseus Distribution
250 West 57th Street
New York, NY 10107

*This book is dedicated to my fellow happy warriors
in the great struggle against eco-lunacy and to anyone else
who believes in truth, liberty, and the scientific method.*

CONTENTS

CONTENTS

A IS FOR AARDVARK

No, not really Aardvark. I just borrowed it for alphabetical convenience so I could explain at the beginning why you might want to buy this book. Here are some reasons:

1. You're an ardent environmentalist who also happens to be an extreme masochist. In which case, this book will take you to heights of ecstasy you had never dreamt possible.

2. You're sick of all the climate change BS from all your greenie friends and colleagues, and you need some ammo to fight back. In which case, this book is like stumbling upon the concealed cache behind the wall in the labyrinth containing the Plasma gun, the Chaingun, the Supershotgun, the Ionized Plasma Levitator, AND the BFG—all at once.

3. You've often wondered about stuff like ocean acidification, just how endangered polar bears really are, whether or not it's true that Rachel Carson was the twentieth century's biggest mass murderer, but have been waiting for a book to come along which is written in a handy, witty, occasionally even humorous A to Z format, so you can read it in short bursts while sitting on the john or maybe give it as a Christmas present or a birthday present to friends who like that kind of thing. In which case, THIS IS THAT BOOK.

A word of warning: it is not comprehensive. If it were, it would have to be called *The Very Enormous Green Book of Eco-Fascism*—perhaps necessitating the strip-harvesting of the entire Amazon Basin or the precious first growth forests of the Pacific Northwest wherein lurks the precious spotted owl.

And we wouldn't want that, would we?

ACID RAIN

We all know that acid rain was one of the great environmental threats of the 1980s—averted thanks to concerted, global government action to reduce sulphur dioxide emissions from power plants. Which just goes to show the power of green propaganda, for in fact, "acid rain" was little more than urban myth, pushed by alarmist environmental journalists such as Fred Pearce, who claimed in 1982 in *New Scientist*: "The forests and lakes are dying. Already the damage may be irreversible."

And the evidence for these claims? As it turned out, little to none. A ten-year U.S. government-sponsored study involving 700 scientists and costing about $500 million said in 1990: "There is no evidence of a general or unusual decline of forests in the United States and Canada due to acid rain." Data from Germany— where the scare originated—told the same story.

A tale, then—as science author Matt Ridley puts it—"not of catastrophe averted but of a minor environmental nuisance somewhat abated."

AEROSOLS

Minute particles added to the atmosphere by burning fossil fuels and which are apparently masking the true extent of runaway climate change. Also known as a handy excuse, trotted out by increasingly desperate Warmists at every opportunity to explain away the failure of their crappy computer models to predict the last sixteen years' non-existent warming.

AGENDA 21

Just because it sounds like a conspiracy theory—like Area 51: the place where *They* keep the alien spaceships which crashed in the Roswell Incident—doesn't mean it's not real.

On the contrary, it's so real that at the 1992 Rio Earth Summit no fewer than 179 nations—Britain and the United States included—signed up to. They did so because, it being a non-binding agreement, they thought it didn't matter.

But that's the evil genius of Agenda 21—the most far-reaching, constrictive, and dangerous environmental code of practice ever devised, yet which looks so harmless and boring that merely reading the first paragraph of its principles acts like super-strength Mogadon.

To wit: "1.1 Humanity stands at a defining moment in history. We are confronted with a perpetuation in disparities between and within nations; a worsening of poverty, hunger, ill-health and illiteracy, and the continuing deterioration of the ecosystems on which we depend for our well being...." Yadda yadda. Zzzzzzz.

Don't be fooled. Even as you read these words some busybody activist group is using Agenda 21 as justification for taking your money, limiting your freedoms, diminishing your living standards—all to achieve the noble goals in that charter I briefly quoted above before you and I both fell asleep.

What's it all about? Pretty much everything you ever hated about pettifogging environmentalist bureaucracy gone mad, basically: zoning restrictions; anti-car measures; climate change initiatives; higher taxes; fines for incorrect recycling; green activists on the local government pay roll as Climate Change officers; public transportation converted—at your expense—to run biofuels; leaflets (paid for by you, again) lecturing you on how to live your life more sustainably.

Agenda 21 is the strategic arm of the sustainable development industry. Its tactical wing—the part that translates its airy precepts into immensely tedious reality—are the Local Agenda 21 (LA21) sub groups which you'll find everywhere from Berkeley, California, to Dallas, Texas, to Finland to Zimbabwe. These groups in turn are coordinated by a UN-funded umbrella group called ICLEI—Local Governments for Sustainability.

Your eyes are glazing over once more. You find all this dull, involved, and wearisome. Of course you do. No sentient person wouldn't. You pay your local government for the basic amenities and services you need—trash disposal, street lighting, road maintenance, etc.—not because you want it to solve Third World poverty, eliminate sexual inequality, combat climate change, address overpopulation, or redistribute income.

Yet, behind the scenes, this is exactly what Agenda 21 is being used to justify.

You didn't vote for it. You weren't consulted. Yet these values—which may be alien to everything you believe in—have now been absorbed, as if by osmosis, to form a key part of your local government's policy.

That's Agenda 21: the blueprint for green tyranny.

ALGORE (*See also* GORE, AL)

A creature we could only wish was mythical—an insufferable, arrogant, sighing-and-eye-rolling, prosperously rotund former-politician-turned-huckster, flying around the world lecturing us on the need to dismantle capitalism for the sake of the planet, while living in a 10,000-square-foot mansion, amassing an enormous fortune of $200 million (in part by selling his leftist TV network to Al Jazeera, a true act of patriotism by one of America's devoted sons), and leaving the carbon footprint of a million farting and frequent-flying abominable snowmen.

AMAZON

 Great big river and accompanying jungle made famous by Sting and other World Saviors; liana-draped, squawking, gibbering, cackling, jaguar-, piranha-, and poison-arrow-frog-infested poster child of the environmental movement; home of that terrible fish—the Candiru—that swims up your urine stream as you pee in the river and lodges itself in your tender organs.

Obviously, it would be really helpful to the green movement's propaganda campaigns if the Amazon really were being wiped out by "global warming." That's why, in their Fourth Assessment report, the Intergovernmental Panel on Climate Change's in-house activists (a.k.a. lead authors) had a seriously good go by announcing that "up to 40 per cent of the Amazonian rainforest" is threatened by climate change.

Problem was there's no actual scientific evidence for this claim. It turned out to have come not from a peer-reviewed study, but from a piece of propaganda literature produced by green activists for the WWF, which made no mention of climate change. That's because the report was about the effects of logging and forest fires.

ANGRY (*See* ROMM, JOE)

ANTHROPOGENIC GLOBAL WARMING (AGW)

Theory, increasingly discredited by real-world evidence, that the planet is warming due to manmade carbon dioxide emissions and that unless we give half our income to renewable energy companies owned by Al Gore, George Soros, or T. Boone Pickens, then we're all going to fry.

Anti-Capitalism

"I think if we don't overthrow capitalism we don't have a chance of saving the world ecologically. I think it is possible to have an ecologically sound society under socialism. I don't think it's possible under capitalism."
—Earth First! member Judi Bari, interviewed 1992.

ARAB SPRING

The Arab Spring violence, which swept across North Africa and the Middle East, began with food riots. And what triggered these food riots? Why, massive food price inflation driven in part by the increasing acreage of land being diverted from agricultural use to biofuels production.

So, to the Eco-Fascists' butcher's bill—along with all the old people they've driven to an early grave through fuel poverty and all the Africans they've starved to death with artificially induced food price inflation—we can perhaps reasonably add the hundreds of thousands slaughtered in the civil unrest from Libya to Syria. Credit where credit's due, eh?

ARCTIC

Dread harbinger of climate change, apparently.

For greenies, the melting Arctic ice cap is a bit like the Seventh Seal: the final sign that all our efforts to save the planet have come to naught and that we are doomed to be consumed by an apocalypse which makes Brueghel's *Triumph of Death* look like Manet's *Le Déjeuner sur l'herbe*. Or, worse, like a scene from Kevin Costner's *Waterworld*.

That is why, at the height of the global warming scare, they frequently sent emissaries to the Arctic circle in order to come back with

A

ever-grimmer tidings with which to terrify any remaining doubters. Sometimes, these took the form of artistic love-ins (see Cape Farewell project), sometimes of pseudo-scientific ventures like the *Catlin Arctic Survey*, and sometimes of intrepid voyages like that undertaken by adventurer and climate campaigner Lewis Pugh, who planned to kayak all the way to the spot where the North Pole would be if it hadn't been melted by global warming....

But they all faced one intractable problem: the Arctic wasn't melting nearly as fast as they hoped it would. Sure, for a tantalizing period it seemed that summer ice melt was almost approaching unprecedented levels. But then, unfortunately, a) it stopped melting quite so much; b) every winter it stubbornly insisted on freezing again; and c) the melting—contrary to the alarmists' claims—turned out to be not unprecedented at all, anyway. As records from the Danish Meteorological Institute show, Arctic mean temperatures have barely changed since its records began in 1958. Other records show that the Arctic was in fact warmer in the 1940s than it is now.

Still, let's not pretend that the melting Arctic ice non-story hasn't had it's beneficial side effects. One or two of us, for example, took the most enormous pleasure in the fact that Lewis Pugh only managed to paddle as far as 81° N before his kayak got trapped in ice; and the fact that the Catlin Arctic Survey expedition had to be abandoned just 434 kilometers into a planned 1,000-kilometer march because their equipment broke in the freezing temperatures, and the weather was just too darn cold.

ANTARCTICA

Another dread harbinger of climate change, apparently.

Antarctica is a godsend for climate alarmists: because it's so big, so remote, so uncharted, they can say whatever they like about how "threatened" it is without fear of contradiction by pesky real world data.

This is how in 2009 a team led by Eric Steig (an associate—*caveat emptor*—of global warming guru Michael Mann) managed to grab headlines by claiming that even the world's coldest continent had fallen prey to global warming.

Steig achieved this using a method popular among climatologists but generally shunned by more mainstream scientists known as "making it up." Or, rather, he relied on computer models, which is much the same thing.

In the models, he combined satellite evidence (which shows that for the last thirty years, at least the Antarctic has been getting colder not warmer) with temperature readings from surface weather stations, plus some estimated (that is, imaginary) temperature readings from non-existent weather stations all over Antarctica whose data he could only guess at.

A more recent paper published in 2013 in *The Cryosphere* finds that, far from warming, Antarctica has been gaining surface ice and snow for at least the past 150 years. But the authors did rather go and spoil it—as is unfortunately the fashion in these credulous times—by blaming the accumulating ice and snow on a "warming climate." Of course!

ASTEROID

> *"Is this an effect of, perhaps, global warming?"*
> —CNN anchor Deb Feyerick introducing a news item
> about an approaching asteroid.

Yeah. That'll be it: a marginal 0.8-degree Celsius increase in global mean temperature since 1850 has made it more likely we're going to be hit by a giant space rock like the one that wiped out the dinosaurs. Oh, and it will also cause the oceans to boil (*see* Astronauts).

Astrologers

"*Perhaps we could start referring to them as astrologers (excusable as 'oops just a typo').*"
—from a "Climategate" email sent by scientist Tom Wigley, discussing ways to smear two scientists who disagree with him, Harvard astronomers Willie Soon and Sallie Balliunas

ASTRONAUTS

In March 2012, nearly fifty former NASA scientists, astronauts, and technologists wrote to protest NASA's position on climate change.

"As former NASA employees, we feel that NASA's advocacy of an extreme position, prior to a thorough study of the possible overwhelming impact of natural climate drivers is inappropriate."

NASA's chief scientist Waleed Abdalati replied: "We support open scientific inquiry and discussion."

Clearly he's never met his colleague James Hansen, former head of NASA's Goddard Institute for Space Studies, who has criticized the "natural skepticism and debates embedded in the scientific process," because it enables chaps like us a look in, and told the U.S. Congress that "CEOs of fossil energy companies know what they are doing and are aware of the long-term consequences of continued business as usual. In my opinion, these CEOs should be tried for high crimes against humanity and nature." Indeed, and perhaps they should be burned to death in our oceans that Hansen predicts will literally boil.

ATTENBOROUGH, DAVID

Gentle, whispery-voiced, gorilla-hugging BBC nature documentary presenter; national treasure; high-profile promulgator of climate change nonsense; neo-Malthusian who wants to kill your kids.

No, of course, nice Sir David Attenborough doesn't really want to kill your kids. Not *your* kids, at any rate. Someone else's, maybe. But definitely not yours.

And he doesn't literally want them to die, of course. He'd just like them to disappear, painlessly, into the ether, as if they'd never been. Something like that, anyway. Not that he has likely ever thought of such unpleasant details. Nice, charming, whispery-voiced, *bien-pensant* types who agonise about the "Overpopulation" issue rarely do.

What we do know is that Sir David—as he told the *Radio Times*—thinks that humans are a "plague on the Earth." And that since 2009, he has been patron of the Optimum Population Trust—an organization which, up until 2011, was quite up front on its website about its goal of reducing the world's then-population of 6.8 billion to a more sustainable 5.1 billion.

Perhaps someone had a quiet word, for the following year the charity changed its name to the slightly less charged Population Matters. It also became less explicit about the number of people it would ideally like wiped from the face of the earth: 1.7 billion really is quite a lot to lose, however kindly and well-intentioned your preferred method of dispatch.

"I've never seen a problem that wouldn't be easier to solve with fewer people—or harder, and ultimately impossible, with more," Sir David told the *Guardian*. Really? So he'd prefer to conduct his filming expeditions to Antarctica or the Congo solo, would he, rather than with a full BBC crew? Or aid missions to impoverished countries that have been hit by tsunamis or hurricanes? They work better, do they, when they're conducted by two men and a dog rather than, say, an aircraft carrier packed with supplies and skilled rescue workers?

AUSTRALIA

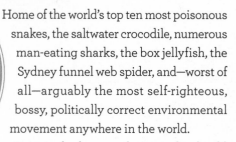

Home of the world's top ten most poisonous snakes, the saltwater crocodile, numerous man-eating sharks, the box jellyfish, the Sydney funnel web spider, and—worst of all—arguably the most self-righteous, bossy, politically correct environmental movement anywhere in the world.

But it is also home to the man who should be the next pope, Cardinal George Pell, archbishop of Sydney, and a level-head global warming skeptic who has said that "some of the more hysterical and extreme claims about global warming appear symptomatic of a pagan emptiness, of a Western fear when confronted by the immense and basically uncontrollable forces of nature.... It's almost as though people without religion ... have got to be frightened of something.... I often point out that some of those who are now warning us against global warming were warning us back in the 1970s about an imminent new ice age, because according to some criteria an ice age is a bit overdue.... Belief in a benign God who is master of the universe has a steadying psychological effect, although it is no guarantee of Utopia, no guarantee that the continuing climate and geographic changes will be benign. In the past pagans sacrificed animals and even humans in vain attempts to placate capricious and cruel gods. Today they demand a reduction in carbon dioxide emissions." Amen, Cardinal Pell, amen.

BACON, FRANCIS (AKA FIRST VISCOUNT ST. ALBAN)

English philosopher, statesman, philosopher, jurist, and author (1561–1626). Your hero.

You may not have realized before that Francis Bacon was your hero—but he is because he stood for almost everything the green movement hates: progress, evidence, knowledge, truth, honesty, civilization, humanity, creature comforts, pleasure.

He is famous for many things: "Knowledge is power"; dying of pneumonia contracted while experimenting with a frozen chicken; but his achievement most relevant to this book is that he is the father of "empiricism" and the "scientific method."

Bacon believed that scientific discovery was important not just for its own sake but in order to improve the lot of mankind. By learning to harness the powers of nature, he believed, we could make our lives less arduous, richer, and freer. The aim of the greenies, of course, is the exact opposite.

BACON, FRANCIS

Dissolute British painter (1909–1992).

Of no relevance whatsoever to this book.

BATS
(See also [BAT-SPLATTING, BIRD-SLICING] ECO-CRUCIFIXES)

Bats are one of the world's most heavily protected species. In Britain, for example, it is actually a *criminal* offense to: deliberately capture, injure, or kill a bat; disturb a bat in its roost; damage a bat roosting place (even if there are no bats there at the time); possess or advertise/sell/ exchange a bat (dead or alive) or any part of a bat; intentionally or recklessly obstruct access to a bat roost.

Has the world gone mad? Well, obviously it has; that's a given. But there is, in this case, at least a glimmer of almost-sanity behind this legislative lunacy: bats—because of their long life cycle and slow breeding cycle—are unusually vulnerable. Kill a breeding pair and you may well have wiped out the bat neighborhood for miles around.

Given that this is so—and known to be so by all conservationists—you've got to ask yourself why the environmental movement isn't united in opposition to the wind industry. Wind turbines are the worst thing to happen to bats in their entire fifty million years on the planet. For some unfortunate reason, (possibly to do with the vibrations) bats are attracted to those spinning blades like moths to a flame—at which point, if they survive the collision, they are killed by the pressure wave which ruptures their internal organs ("barotraumized") and causes them to drop from the night sky like stones.

Every year, in the United States alone, an estimated 28,470,000 bats are splatted by wind turbines. (That's based on a fairly conservative estimate of two bat deaths per turbine per day.) So why, you might wonder, aren't the tree-huggers kicking up more of a stink? Why aren't the greenies marching on D.C. with their "Save the Bat" placards to demand that subsidies to the wind industry (the only reason anyone would bother erecting these hideous, noisy, bat-splatting eco-crucifixes in the first place) be slashed to zero, forthwith?

Why indeed. Here is a perfect illustration of the cognitive dissonance at the very heart of the green psychopathology. In the environmentalist mindset, wind power is "clean," eco-friendly, and morally right; therefore, when strong evidence emerges that wind power is none of those things, the only response of which the greenies are capable is to stick a finger in each ear and go "Nyah, nyah, nyah. Not listening."

BBC

The Truth about Climate Change; *Climate Change: Britain Under Threat*; *Meltdown: A Global Warming Journey*; *Climate Wars*; *Horizon: Science Under Attack?*; a dedicated climate change episode of *Frozen Planet*; a *Climate Chaos* season in which children's favorite Blue Peter was rechristened Green Peter; an evening news bulletin declaring: "At 6 o'clock—no more doubt. Climate Change is happening—and we are to blame"; a music drama, especially commissioned for the BBC Proms concerts, inspired by Hurricane Katrina about children lost after a storm caused by climate change; a BBC *Panorama* episode, "What's Up with the Weather?"; *Burn Up* (a drama about global warming); *Horizon: Global Weirding*....

Just a few examples of the kind of measured contribution to the debate on global warming the British viewer can expect from the national broadcaster in return for his compulsory $200 annual license fee.

And the number of programs on the BBC in the last fifteen years expressing a skeptical position on climate change?

Try: Zero. Nada. Zip. None.

BEDTIME STORIES (*See also* KIDS)

In 2009, the British government's Department of Energy and Climate Change spent £6 million on probably the most mendacious state propaganda campaign since the ones they ran in the eighties claiming we were all going to die of AIDS.

The highlight was a TV commercial where a cute little girl is shown being read a bedtime story by her father.

"Scientists said it was being caused by too much CO_2 which went into the sky

B

when the grown-ups used energy. They said it was getting dangerous. Its effects were happening faster than they thought. Some places could even disappear under the sea. And it was the children of the land who'd have to live with the horrible consequences...."

As the father turns the pages, we see the girl frowning at the increasingly scary illustrations: a great big, razor-toothed carbon monster ravages the land; a cartoon cat floating on an upturned table reaches out in vain to save a drowning cartoon puppy.... It is all too, too real, isn't it?

"BEYOND PETROLEUM"

Cynical, morally obscene, counterproductive greenwashing exercise conducted by BP in 2001 to persuade people it was no longer "just" about oil.

Cynical because it obviously still was an oil company: at the time of the rebranding, it had just swallowed up three large oil concerns.

Morally obscene because to compensate for the massive losses it made on its green investments—including a disastrous venture into solar power—it had to cut costs on its regular operations, leading to the lax safety standards which resulted in the Deepwater Horizon drilling rig explosion in the Gulf of Mexico.

Counterproductive because the punitive damages inflicted on BP as a result of Deepwater Horizon ran into the billions.

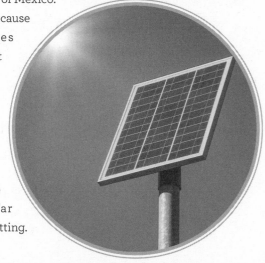

When is capitalism going to learn? If you try to appease the green enemy by playing by their rules, you're never going to win. Far better to stick to your knitting.

There's nothing wrong with petroleum. It's why God made dinosaurs and other beasts and plants of prehistory. It's biodiversity at work!

BIG GREEN

- Number of environmental groups in the United States (as of 2005): 26,500

- Annual spending of the top fifty of those groups (2005): $4.98 billion

- Estimated total annual spending of all those groups: $9.7 billion

- Annual U.S. federal and state government spending on environmental projects: $44.5 billion

- Annual budget paid by Western nations since 1992 Rio Earth Summit to sustainable development funds: $68 billion

- Amount given by Environmental Protection Agency in past ten years to green activist groups: $3 billion

- Amount of President Obama's stimulus spent on green projects: $78.6 billion

- Estimated corporate spending in the United States and Canada on "sustainable business" by 2014: $70 billion

- Estimate corporate spending within European Union on "sustainable business" by 2014: $97.98 billion

(Figures from *Eco-Fascists* by Elizabeth Nickson)

BIN LADEN, OSAMA

Environmentalist.

Dubai (AFP), January 2010—al Qaeda chief Osama bin Laden lectured the United States and other industrial nations on climate change and urged a dollar boycott in response to American "slavery," in a fresh verbal assault broadcast Friday.

In the message aired on Al Jazeera television, possibly timed to coincide with the World Economic Forum in Davos, bin Laden said, "all industrial nations, mainly the big ones, are responsible for the crisis of global warming."

"Discussing climate change is not an intellectual luxury, but a reality," he said in the audio recording whose authenticity could not be immediately verified.

"This is a message to the whole world about those who are causing climate change, whether deliberately or not, and what we should do about that."

Biodiversity

As most people understand it: a cornucopia of twittering birds, fluttering butterflies, hoppity bunny rabbits, lions, tigers, and every tree or flower or bug you could possibly imagine, all merrily coexisting in a thriving, healthy, unspoilt world of Eden-like abundance.

As environmentalists understand it: another handy excuse for regulation, wealth redistribution, taxation, banning all commercial enterprise, sequestration by experts with khaki shirts and degrees in conservation biology, the assumption that humans are a less helpful, useful part of biodiversity than are dung beetles.

BIOFUELS

Ingenious green scheme whereby rainforests are replaced by palm oil plantations, and agricultural land is given over to ethanol production in order to protect the world from the deadly threat of plant food (a.k.a. CO_2).

For environmentalists who support biofuels, it's a win-win-win: orangutans and other rainforest creatures are killed and displaced,

meaning more money for the World Wildlife Fund; indigenous jungle peoples are displaced, meaning more money for Survival International; ethanol mandates drive up the price of fuel, meaning more misery for evil car-driving capitalists; they also create food shortages in the Third World, thus helping to solve the Overpopulation (q.v.) problem.

B

BIRD FLU

Deadly viral menace which, according to the World Health Organization's official forecast, would result in between two million and 7.4 million dead. Bird flu, claimed a UN official in 2005, is "like a combination of global warming and HIV/AIDS 10 times faster than it's running at the moment."

Approximate total death toll of bird flu before it disappeared in around 2007: 200 dead.

BLIND SALMON AND RABBITS
(*See also* OZONE LAYER)

> "In Patagonia, hunters now report finding blind rabbits;
> fishermen catch blind salmon."
> —Al Gore, *Earth In Balance*

Gore attributed this to ozone depletion over southern Chile caused—of course—by evil man and his wanton use of underarm deodorant and

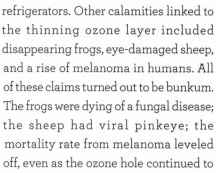

refrigerators. Other calamities linked to the thinning ozone layer included disappearing frogs, eye-damaged sheep, and a rise of melanoma in humans. All of these claims turned out to be bunkum. The frogs were dying of a fungal disease; the sheep had viral pinkeye; the mortality rate from melanoma leveled off, even as the ozone hole continued to grow; the mystery of the blind rabbits and salmon remained a mystery, but they might have been blinded by the fierce, hot air, something like a global Sirocco, blowing from Al Gore.

BLOGOSPHERE

If it weren't for the Blogosphere, you wouldn't be reading this book. Well, you might, but it would be called something like *Lovely, Decent Greenies: A Pocket Celebration of the Wit, Wisdom, and Total Rightness of the Warm, Caring Environmental Movement.*

That's because, if you're looking for criticism of environmentalism anywhere outside the internet, you can pretty much forget it. Sure, there's the odd skeptical outpost—Canada's *National Post*; Britain's *Mail, Express,* and *Sunday Telegraph*; the *Wall Street Journal*; the *Australian*—but for the most part, the old print media fell to the Orcish green hordes long ago. As, too, did most of the TV channels from CNBC to the BBC to ABC.

How did this happen? What prompted the mainstream media to abandon all pretense of objectivity and decide to report on arguably the most contentious and far-reaching political issue of the age, with all the starry-eyed credulousness and hard-left bias of a brown-rice, tofu, and species-extinction seminar at the World Wildlife Fund?

Perhaps we'll never know. What we can say with confidence though is that the public at large wouldn't have even nearly so well-informed about the true nature of the debate if it hadn't been for websites like

Climate Audit, Watts Up with That, Jo Nova, No Frakking Consensus, Bishop Hill, No Tricks Zone, Tallbloke's Talkshop, Small Dead Animals, and Ecotretas, to name but a few of the sceptical websites, large and small, across the world from Australia to Portugal, Canada to Germany, Britain to the United States, including the humble postings of one Delingpole, James, on a blog at the online *Daily Telegraph*.

Not since Gutenberg invented the printing press, perhaps, has the cause of openness and liberty made so spectacular a leap as it has as a result of the internet. And for much the same reasons. Before the printing press, knowledge—and, by extension, power—was the preserve of a self-serving, self-perpetuating elite. Afterwards, this jealously guarded information suddenly became free to a much wider and less reverential audience.

So it has been with the internet. No longer can the likes of Phil Jones and Michael Mann conceal their dodgy dealings behind the bastions of academe. Not in an age where an amateur sleuth such as Steve McIntyre now has the freedom to double-check their research, find it sorely wanting, and spread the news far and wide. So blog on!

CAMERON, JAMES

Movie director, environmental activist, best known for his epic *Avatar*, a.k.a. *Dances with Smurfs.*

"We are devastating habitat and biodiversity at a terrible rate. We are causing a global climate change that's going to be absolutely devastating to the coral reefs." Wow! Big-budget, blockbuster, epic-action movie directors: Is there *anything* they don't know about the environment?

CANADA

Formerly: joke nation; "gentle giant" to the north of the United States; spawning ground for leftist One World Government fetishists such as Pierre Trudeau and Maurice Strong.

Today: the Helm's Deep of Western civilization; spawning ground of mighty, climate-skeptic heroes like Steve McIntyre, Ross McKitrick, Terence Corcoran, Lawrence Solomon, Ezra Levant, Tim Ball, et al.; fearless defender of cheap energy and free markets against the green hordes, as shown by its unapologetic exploitation of its tar sands—now ingeniously rebranded "ethical oil."

CARBON CAPTURE AND SEQUESTRATION (CCS) (*See also* BIOFUELS; CARBON TRADING; ETC.)

Hare-brained, eye-wateringly expensive, and unproven technology whereby CO_2 released from fossil fuel power stations is captured and buried beneath the ground.

Despite the expenditure of billions of dollars of taxpayers' money in the United States on this thrillingly pointless scheme to bury millions of metric tons of CO_2 beneath the soil, thus turning a harmless form of plant food into something potentially very dangerous, CCS has failed wherever it has been tried.

A 2010 U.S. government report found that to store the CO_2 released by an average-sized fossil fuel power station would require reservoir space the size of a small U.S. state. Risks include pressure buildup and leakage.

So, possibly, the craziest green solution yet. Apart from all the other crazy green solutions.

CARBON TRADING

In 2011, the global Carbon Market Trading climbed to $176 billion. This made it worth about the same as total global wheat production in that year.

Wheat provides about 20 percent of the calories consumed by the seven billion people on the planet.

Carbon trading produces nothing of value to anyone.

Is there any better example of the madness that has afflicted our world in the name of environmentalism?

CARSON, RACHEL

Poster girl for the modern environmental movement; Al Gore's inspiration; author of *Silent Spring*; mass murderer.

Considering she was so wrong about everything, Rachel Carson has been treated well by posterity. Several wildlife reserves have been named after her, as have at least one school, a bridge, a hiking trail, and three environmental prizes, while her birthplace in Springdale,

Pennsylvania, is on the National Register of Historic Places. Every year, a "sustainable" feast is held there in her honor.

Quite an achievement, really, for a junk scientist, scaremonger, and fabulist who has not altogether unreasonably been accused of being one of the twentieth century's most prolific mass murderers.

The title depends on the degree to which she stands culpable for the near worldwide ban on DDT. We shall never know how many people in the developing world died needlessly of malaria as a result, but it certainly runs into the millions.

Then again, if you share Rachel Carson's ecological worldview—in which man is but one species among many—maybe that's not such a problem.

"In truth, man is against the earth," she once wrote to a friend.

So really, all those deaths were just payback time.

Catastrophic Anthropogenic Global Warming (CAGW)

When it became clear that man-made global warming in itself isn't a problem, someone added the "C" to make it sound more scary. Nice idea. Pity there's no evidence to support it.

"CHEAPER THAN OIL/GAS/COAL/ EVERYTHING"

Periodic lie—regurgitated in cod-economic reports produced by green industry fellow travelers like Bloomberg New Energy Finance—that renewable energy works out cheaper than fossil fuel.

Yes, renewable energy is cheaper than fossil fuels ... but only if you completely ignore the massive taxpayer subsidies and hidden levies paid to renewable energy producers; or, if you make heroically fantastical assumptions about a) how steeply fossil fuel prices are going to rise, and b) how massively renewable energy prices are going to fall due to advances in technology, economies of scale, magical fairies appearing from the skies to blow those turbine blades 'round extra hard, etc.

Ain't gonna happen.

Ever.

CHECK IN THE MAIL
(*See* GREEN JOBS)

CHEMOTHERAPY FOR A COLD

- Estimated cost of reducing global manmade CO_2 emissions 50 percent by 2050—according to the International Energy Agency (in 2008)—$45 trillion

- Conclusive evidence that global manmade CO_2 emissions are a problem—zero

- Estimated amount of money therefore wasted "combating climate change"—$45 trillion

Matt Ridley has described this as being like using "chemotherapy to cure a cold." But actually it's worse than that: the cold being cured doesn't even exist.

CHERNOBYL
(*See also* FUKUSHIMA; PLUTONIUM; SIMPSON, HOMER)

Excuse routinely trotted out by greenies to justify their religious aversion to nuclear power.

Here are the facts according to 2005's The Chernobyl Forum, an investigation conducted over two years by eight UN-specialized agencies including the International Atomic Energy Agency (IAEA) and the World Health Organization (WHO—not a body generally known for underplaying health scares):

- Fewer than fifty deaths are directly attributable to radiation from the disaster. Most of these were highly exposed rescue workers.

- No profound negative health impacts to the population in surrounding areas.

- No widespread contamination that would continue to pose a substantial health risk except in a few restricted areas.

- About 4,000 cases of thyroid cancer with a survival rate approaching 99 percent.

- No evidence or likelihood of decreased fertility in the affected population, nor of increases in congenital malformations.

- Other than thyroid cancer, no increases in cancer rates in the affected regions.

CHICAGO CLIMATE EXCHANGE (CCX)

Carbon trading exchange set up in 2000 to capitalize on the thriving industry in carbon credits and other green trading mechanisms. Closed in 2010 after that thriving industry never quite materialized. But not before early investors including (who else?) Goldman Sachs and (who else?) Al Gore had made their lucrative exit. The biggest winner was economist Richard Sandor who dreamt up the idea and came away with a cool $90 million. And quite right, too: it takes real genius to persuade that many hard-headed businessmen to invest that much money in a business whose *raison d'être* is to trade an invisible product no one wants or needs and which could only possibly ever survive within a watertight regulatory regime run by the kind of One World Government which currently only exists as a twinkle in George Soros's sinister red eyes.

CLEAN AIR ACT

"Free markets need regulation. Without it, what would stop businesses polluting everything?"

Hard-wired into the green mindset is an instinctive mistrust of human nature. The only reason people will ever behave well is if they're compelled to do so by a—presumably—benign and all-knowing state. But is this actually true?

What Julian Simon once famously showed in a debate with environmental activist Hazel Henderson is that the natural tendency of industrial civilization—regardless of government intervention—is toward a cleaner environment.

In the debate, Henderson produced a graph to show how London's 1956 Clean Air Act had effected a remarkable improvement in the city's pollution record: and there, for all to see, was the downward sloping line to prove it.

Simon responded by pulling out a chart of his own, this one stretching much further back—to the 1800s—and with a line from the 1920s showing a constant and uniform downward slope.

"If you look at the data you can't tell there was a Clean Air Act at any point," he said.

The same, incidentally, is true in the United States. Most major air pollutants had been declining prior to the Federal Clean Air Act of 1970.

Capitalist prosperity means cleaner air—except in China where, not coincidentally, Communists control the market.

Clean Energy

Green euphemism for expensive, environmentally destructive, heavily taxpayer-subsidized, piddling, unreliable "renewable" energy.

CLIMATE CENTRAL (*See also* DRAWBRIDGE EFFECT; GOOGLE)

Website dedicated to junk-science fearmongering—along the lines of *"Seas will rise, flood millions of homes,"* warns ecologist—funded by Google.org and by the Schmidt Family Foundation (as in Google founder Eric Schmidt).

CLIMATEGATE

Do you think it's okay for scientists to lie, cheat, smear, bully, bury inconvenient data, twist evidence, breach freedom of information laws, destroy the careers of dissenting colleagues, misuse public money, abuse the scientific method, and impede the path of scientific progress?

If your answer is "yes" then you're in excellent, high-level company. Among those who agree with you are: Sir Paul Nurse, president of the Royal Society; Dr. James Hansen, adjunct professor at Columbia University; Elizabeth May, head of Canada's Green Party; Professor Myles Allen of Oxford University; Professor Kerry Emanuel of MIT; the *Guardian*; the *New York Times*; the Prince of Wales; Al Gore; the BBC; ABC; NBC; the National Academy of Sciences; Dr. Rajendra Pachauri, head of the Intergovernmental Panel on Climate Change; the European Union; the United Nations; and no fewer than four official inquiries.

If your answer's "no," then you'll probably be unconvinced by the above experts' claims that Climategate was just a case of "Move along. Nothing to see here." Indeed, you might even decide that Climategate represents the greatest scientific scandal of our age.

The story broke in November 2009 when, on the eve of the Copenhagen climate summit, a mysterious whistleblower (later calling himself FOIA) leaked onto the internet a cache of private emails and other computer data from the Climatic Research Unit (CRU) at the University of East Anglia (UEA).

This mattered because the CRU is one of the most important climate research establishments in the world, on whose data, opinions, and supposed expertise the future of the global economy depends. On the word of scientists at the CRU—and sister organizations such as NASA's Goddard Institute for Space Studies, where James Hansen used to hang his hat—governments around the world have spent trillions of dollars of our money trying to deal with the apparently urgent and unprecedented threat of Catastrophic Anthropogenic Global Warming. So imagine if that "threat" were suddenly exposed as, at best, exaggerated; at worst, illusory.

Imagine no more for that is exactly what the Climategate emails revealed. Instead of behaving like dispassionate seekers-after-truth, the scientists in these emails were caught red-handed behaving like political activists. They've already made up their minds about Man-Made Global Warming. And if the evidence doesn't actually support their shaky hypothesis then, damn it, they'll torture it till it does.

Hence the infamous Michael Mann "Hide the Decline [in temperatures]" (q.v.) email. And the one where true believer Kevin Trenberth exclaims in frustration: "The fact is that we can't account for the lack of warming at the moment and it is a travesty that we can't." And the ones showing how these shysters deal with scientists foolish enough to disagree with them: not through rational debate, but trying to get them sacked or to have the journals which publish their work closed down.

Apologists for Climategate will often try to persuade you that the emails were "cherry-picked" or taken out of context or just a case of ordinary, decent scientists engaged in the rough-and-tumble of honest scientific research. The emails show no such thing. What they reveal is that the scientists who've been scaring us for the last two decades with terrifying tales of a man-made climate apocalypse simply cannot be trusted. The entire edifice of the great global warming scam is built on a foundation of lies, corruption, and junk science.

CLIMATEGATE INQUIRIES (*See* JOKE; WHITEWASH)

CLUB OF ROME

Shadowy organization which you read about on the internet and which you think can't possibly exist because it sounds so darned sinister and evil; best known for its 1972 bestseller, *Limits to Growth*.

Since its foundation in the late 1960s, the membership of the Club of Rome (and its sister organizations the Club of Budapest and the Club of Madrid) has swollen to include the Dalai Lama, Al Gore, Kofi Annan, Bill Clinton, Mikhail Gorbachev, Deepak Chopra, Bianca Jagger, and Peter Gabriel.

Here is their organization's Master Plan—and they really do call it this, without apparently being embarrassed that this is the phrase normally used only by cat-stroking villains in James Bond movies—as described in their 1993 publication, *The First Global Revolution*.

"Now is the time to draw up a master plan for organic, sustainable growth and world development based on allocation of scarce resources and a new global economic system."

Who voted for this stuff? No one did. That's the point. If people like you are given any choice in the matter, you'll almost certainly opt for the wrong thing. That's why you need this wise über-elite of self-appointed chosen ones to make the right decisions for you: the guy from Genesis who used to dress up as a flower; the girl who used to be married to Mick Jagger; the author of *Teens Ask Deepak* and *Synchrodestiny: Harnessing the Infinite Power of Coincidence to Create Miracles*. They'll know what to do....

CONNOLLEY, WILLIAM

Green party activist who "turned *Wikipedia* into the missionary wing of the global warming movement."

Between 2003 and 2009, Connolley created or rewrote 5,428 unique *Wikipedia* articles, caused another 500 articles he disapproved of to disappear, had more than 2,000 *Wikipedia* contributors who ran afoul of him blocked from making further contributions, almost erased *Wikipedia* entries for the Little Ice Age and the Medieval Warming Period, dissed skeptical scientists like Fred Singer and Richard Lindzen, and bigged up the work of alarmists like Michael Mann to the point where even today you'd scarcely guess, reading his entry, that this man was responsible for one of the most widely discredited artifacts—the Hockey Stick (q.v.)—in junk science history.

CONSENSUS? WHAT CONSENSUS?

"97 per cent of climate scientists" believe in man-made global warming. Have you ever wondered where they got that figure? Let me tell you: a 2009 online poll of scientists—the Doran Survey—conducted by two researchers at the University of Illinois.

They asked two questions:

- When compared with pre-1800s levels, do you think that mean global temperatures have generally risen, fallen, or remained relatively constant?

- Do you think human activity is a significant contributing factor in changing mean global temperatures?

To both of which questions, even most skeptics would answer "yes." The only room for dissent would be over that term "significant."

But even with such carefully loaded questions the researchers were disappointed by the lack of unanimity of response from the more than 10,000 scientists they originally surveyed. So, in order to stack the odds still further in their favor, they decided to exclude all save the respondents who self-identified as "climate scientists."

Even here, after reducing their 10,000 scientists to fewer than one hundred, their respondents were incapable of achieving full consensus. But it was near enough: seventy-five out of a total of seventy-seven "climate scientists" agreed with a premise that even skeptics might accept. Remember that next time someone quotes that "97 per cent" statistic at you—and maybe take the opportunity to explain why you're less impressed by this figure than they'd like you to be.

Conservation Biology

Branch of politicized junk-science devised at the University of California, San Diego, in the 1970s in order to demonstrate that man is the problem, resources are finite, and that something must be done—and soon—preferably by employing as many conservation biologists as the state can afford.

CONSPIRACY THEORIST (*See also* DENIER)

Mad, crazy, whacked-out fruit loop who suspects that Al Gore, Dr. Michael Mann, the World Wildlife Fund, Greenpeace, Goldman Sachs, grant-hungry climate scientists, the renewable energy industry, the insurance companies, the United Nations, the European Union, the EPA, the Obama administration, the Intergovernmental Panel on Climate Change, the Climatic Research Unit at the University of East Anglia, Dr. James Hansen, and others might possibly have an ulterior motive in promoting the biggest scientific scare story in history, for which there is no hard evidence but which will bring to those who jump on the bandwagon enormous power and/or vast personal gain.

CORPORATE SOCIAL RESPONSIBILITY (CSR)

Job creation scheme for otherwise unemployable law and social sciences graduates. Oil companies, for example, keep tame environmental sciences graduates on inflated salaries in order to demonstrate to the world that their industry has nothing whatsoever to do with extracting viscous, dirty hydrocarbons from the womb of Mother Gaia but is, in fact, wholly dedicated to trees, flowers, bees, and fluffy bunny rabbits.

CRAB LICE

According to the World Wildlife Fund, the variety of species that become extinct every year could number in the tens of thousands.

"Unlike the mass extinction events of geological history, the current extinction challenge is one for which a single species—ours—appears to be almost wholly responsible."

This is terrible. So why isn't the WWF doing more to protect a species which, thanks to fickle fashion, is being driven by mankind to the brink of extinction?

- Its natural habitat is being ruthlessly eradicated in waxing parlors around the world.

- Numbers are plummeting especially in the United States, where more than 80 percent of female college students now engage in some form of auto-deforestation.

- In Australia, Sydney's main sexual health clinic reports that it has not seen a single specimen since 2008.

- The genocide was initiated in Manhattan in a salon run by seven Brazilian sisters, whose nationality gave this murderous technique its name.

Yes, the Brazilian bikini wax is destroying the world's population of *Phtirus pubis*—a.k.a. pubic lice; a.k.a. crabs. Yet no one seems to care, least of all the callous WWF.

At best, they stand accused of being outrageous hypocrites; at worst, of abominable speciesism.

Personally, I shall not be giving another cent to the panda charity until their chief executive Carter Roberts steps forward and does the decent thing. He must offer up his body as a human wildlife sanctuary so as to preserve this most underrated of species for the benefit of future generations.

C

DAMON, MATT

Movie star, environmental activist, rose to worldwide fame in 2004 thanks to by far the most animated, moving, and credible performance of his career in *Team America*.

Sadly, since *Team America*, Damon's career has taken a dive—most recently with the disastrous anti-fracking movie *The Promised Land*. Damon, who wrote, produced, and starred in the movie, claimed to have been entirely unaware that one of its financiers, Image Nation, was owned by an oil-rich Middle Eastern nation (United Arab Emirates), which has a keen interest in promoting a global anti-fracking narrative. "The first time we were aware that Image Nation was involved was when we saw the rough cut and saw their logo," claimed producer Damon.

D

DDT

"In a little more than two decades, DDT has prevented 500 million deaths that would otherwise have been inevitable," concluded the National Academy of Sciences in 1965. DDT—dichlorodiphenyltrichloroethane—was and remains one of the world's most effective insecticides, more than proving its worth in the battle against malaria.

Why then, in 1970, did the first head of the EPA William Ruckelshaus decide it should be banned in the United States—leading many other countries 'round the world to do likewise as a result of activist pressure?

Not for any factual reasons, certainly. As the presiding judge concluded after the seven-month EPA hearing: "DDT is not a carcinogenic hazard to man…. DDT is not a mutagenic or teratogenic hazard to man.... The use of DDT under the regulations involved here do not have a deleterious effect on freshwater fish, estuarine organisms, wild birds, or other wildlife."

Nope. DDT was banned for much the same reasons CO_2 has now become the environmental movement's public enemy number one: scientifically groundless scaremongering, in DDT's case prompted by the junk science claims in Rachel Carson's bestseller *Silent Spring*.

The global banning—or near-banning—of DDT remains one of the most grievous stains on the modern environmental movement's con-science, resulting as it did in millions of otherwise preventable deaths from malaria.

What's amusing—or disgusting, depending on your cynicism and tolerance threshold—is the way the greenies in online forums tend to answer this charge. "It's an absolute nonsense that there was ever a worldwide ban on DDT," they'll insist—quite correctly, but rather miss-ing the point. For, isn't that a bit like defending Mao on the pernicious charge that fifty million died as result of his famine, by insisting testily: "It was 49.5 million, at most...."?

Death Train (*See also* DENIER)

Term used by the never-knowingly understated Dr. James Hansen to describe any train carrying coal to a power station. Any connec-tion with the hideously cramped, insanitary cattle trucks which transported six million Jews to the concentration camps of Aus-chwitz, Treblinka, and Sobibor was, presumably, wholly uninten-tional on his part.

DEFINITION OF A "GREEN JOB" ACCORDING TO THE OBAMA ADMINISTRATION

In 2008, presidential candidate Barack Obama promised to create five million "green jobs." In 2012, by some estimates, no more than 910 of these had actually materialized. But, of course, it depends what your definition of a "green job" is. Under questioning from Darrell Issa, House Oversight Committee chairman, a senior U.S. Labor Department official was coaxed into revealing the government's generous definition of the term.

It included: bus drivers; bicycle repair shop employees; antique dealers; thrift shop workers; rare book and manuscript sellers; teenage kids who work in used record shops; railroad rolling stock manufacturers; trash disposal workers; oil lobbyists.

DELINGPOLE, JAMES

Climate denier; Antichrist; murderer of future generations; capitalist shill in the pay of Big Oil, Big Carbon, Big Evil, the Koch Brothers, and the Heartland Institute. Supplements his immense personal fortune by telling evil lies about the environment in the *Spectator* (UK version), the *Telegraph, Ricochet, Human Events*, and the *Wall Street Journal*. Also, a quite clever novelist and author of the nonfiction classic *Welcome to Obamaland*, which Americans ignored to their peril in reelecting Barack Obama.

DEMOCATASTROPHE

"Some of us are now drawn to believe that a demo-catastrophe will be an eco-bonanza. In other words, a population readjustment on a planetary scale from 4,000 million to something in the nature of 200 million would be the only possible solution for the survival of the eco-system or systems that nurtured us."

—John Aspinall, 1960s society-gambler-turned-millionaire zoo owner; keen conservationist; lost five of his keepers to his exotic pets (two killed by elephants; three by tigers); 200 million, incidentally, is about the size of the population of Brazil

Democracy

> "*Democracy is not a panacea. It cannot organise every-*
> *thing and is unaware of its own limits. These facts must*
> *be faced squarely. Sacrilegious though this may sound,*
> *democracy is no longer well suited to the tasks ahead.*
> *The complexity and the technical nature of many of*
> *today's problems do not always allow elected representa-*
> *tives to make competent decisions at the right time.*"
> —Club of Rome (q.v.), 1993

DENIER (*See also* CONSPIRACY THEORIST; DEATH TRAIN)

Mysterious term used by environmentalists to describe climate skeptics. But what exactly is it that we're denying?

That climate changes? But we're all agreed on that: it's been doing
so for the last 4.5 billion years.

That man has an influence on global climate? But we're agreed on
that, too: everything from the Urban Heat Island effect to anthropogenic
CO_2 to the animals we breed for food plays a role in climate change.

That spending trillions of dollars on an unproven (and unlikely)
theory is a great way to use up scarce resources? Ah. Now, that one we
DO deny.

One thing's for certain: no way would those well-meaning environmentalists be using the "denier" word in order to make out that being a
climate skeptic puts you in the same camp as those nutjobs that deny
that Hitler murdered six million Jews. That would be wrong, under-
handed, misleading—and in truly terrible taste, surely?

Still, just be sure, let's see what George Monbiot has to say on the
subject. He's an environmentalist. He's bound to know.

And here he is, writing in the *Guardian* in 2006: "Almost everywhere
climate change denial now looks as stupid and unacceptable as Holocaust denial."

Whoops!

D

DENMARK

Home of LEGO, Bjorn Lomborg, but not of people with horns on their helmets. That stuff about Vikings having horns on their helmets, as any reenactor will tell you, it's historically inaccurate.

Denmark has more wind turbines per capita than any nation on earth. And also the most expensive electricity of any nation on Earth. Gosh, I wonder what the connection might be?

DESERTIFICATION

Yet further proof that the greenies are wrong about everything—especially the thing they're supposed to be experts in: conservation.

Desertification is a genuine environmental problem: all around the world—from

the United States and Canada to Australia, Africa, and China—vast areas of grassland are turning into barren desert. And of course if you listen to the greenies on this, they will tell you—as ever—that it's all man's fault. Their preferred solution is to encourage us all to eat less meat (so that more agricultural land can be set aside) and to sequester land in vast conservation areas from which livestock is banished. This is because they think the problem is overgrazing, which leads to dust-bowls.

In fact, though, the opposite is true. As Zimbabwe-born rancher and range scientist Allan Savory (of the Savory Institute) argues, what grasslands need to survive are large numbers of cloven-hoofed animals (such as migrating caribou and buffalo) breaking up and fertilizing the soil in order to allow it to regenerate. By mimicking this with domestic livestock, modern agriculturalists can heal the land. The real problem, in other words, is not overgrazing but undergrazing. To see this in action, visit the Savory Institute's website and look at the photograph of two farmsteads in South Africa, one carrying one animal to eighteen hectares, the other carrying one animal to twenty-eight hectares. Which one do you think has the lusher, more abundant grassland: the most densely populated, heavily grazed one, or the other? You'll be surprised....

DICAPRIO, LEONARDO

Movie star, environmental activist, achieved worldwide fame thanks to his appearance on the cover of *Vanity Fair*'s 2007 green issue with ursine pin-up megastar Knut (q.v.), the (now sadly deceased) polar bear cub.

No. Leo does not have a bijou, white, real bearskin rug in his eco-chic, Battery Park City condo. It's lies, I tell you. Lies!

DOG POOP YOGURT FALLACY

"There is a difference between a healthy skepticism toward liberal shibboleths and dogmatic resistance to accumulated evidence."
—Michael Gerson and Peter Wehner from an article called "How to Save the Republican Party"; *Commentary*, March 2013

All too often, gutless, principle-lite politicians, cynical strategists, and wishy-washy columnists will try to persuade you that the answer always lies in the center ground. The above quote from the (normally reliably conservative) *Commentary* magazine is a case in point. In order to make themselves more electable, the authors argue, what Republicans must do is adopt a more "reasonable" position on "climate disruption" and "combating climate change" in order to "show that they are not, in fact, at war with the scientific method."

The best reply to this is what I call the Dog Poop Yogurt Fallacy. It goes like this:

Some people like fruit in their yogurt. Cherry, maybe. Raspberry or strawberry. I myself am rather partial to apricot.

But there's another kind of person who thinks that fruit in yogurt belongs to the age of decadence, greed, and unhealthy overconsumption. What we should be adding to our yogurt now, they believe, is something more in tune with our changing times and the needs of future generation. Something more earthy, organic, sustainable, abundant, and recycled. Dog poop, these new agers believe, is the answer.

"No way! That is beyond disgusting," say the fruit-adding traditionalists.

"Greedy capitalist, too selfish to change your lifestyle!" reply the dog-poopers, accusingly.

"No wait, I've got a great idea," says the disinterested, third party. (Maybe a RINO squish columnist in the fine traditions of David Brooks; or an eco-friendly "capitalist" like Mayor Bloomberg; or a "Republican" like Arnie Schwarzenegger.) "How about we compromise? How about we find the middle way? How about from henceforward we all eat our yogurt with a little bit of fruit in it and a little bit of dog poop in it?"

Yeah, right. That'll work.

DRAWBRIDGE EFFECT

Why do so many movie stars champion the kind of environmental campaigns designed to make energy more expensive, land less affordable, taxes higher? Why are some of the most aggressively anti-capitalist environmental foundations the creation of entrepreneurs and industrialists who made their fortunes out of capitalism?

It has to do with the "drawbridge effect": once they've gotten rich, the very last thing these people want to be reminded of is where they came from, let alone spend time in the company of ordinary people like

they used to be. That's why, when they've built their castles and surrounded them with a moat the final thing they do is pull up the drawbridge.

There are other reasons, too. Consider the Pew Foundation—the most vigorous campaigner against Canada's oil sands. And how did the Pew family make all their money? Why, out of the oil business, through a company formerly called Sun Oil and now called Sunoco.

And how does Sunoco continue to make part of its profits? By refining the tar sands oil, which the Pew Foundation claims to find so objectionable.

Is there a conflict of interest here, given that seven of the twelve board members of the Pew Charitable Trusts are either Pew family heirs to the Sunoco fortune or the former CEO? Not nearly as much as you might think.

First, the Pew heirs get to salve their environmental consciences even as they reap the profits from "dirty oil"; second, they get to greenwash their company's image; third, the extra regulation that Pew's activities help generate might well shut down smaller competitors.

DYSON, FREEMAN

British-born, U.S.-resident theoretical physicist, professor, and mathematician; generally held to be one of the world's greatest scientists—as confirmed by the Nobel committee's ongoing failure to award him a prize.

On "global warming": "I'm not saying the warming doesn't cause problems, obviously it does. Obviously we should be trying to understand it. I'm saying that the problems are being grossly exaggerated. They take away money and attention from other problems that are much more urgent and important. Poverty, infectious diseases, public educa-tion and public health. Not to mention the preservation of living crea-tures on land and in the oceans."

Chalk him up as a skeptic. Which means if you are, too, you're in some pretty high-level company.

D

EARTH DAY: HOW IT SAVED THE WORLD

Earth Day was founded in 1970 by Senator Gaylord Nelson to raise global awareness of environmental issues. It was an instant success: twenty million Americans participated in the first one—a million of them (including celebrity guests Paul Newman and Ali McGraw) at a rally in Central Park, New York.

Here (with thanks to Washington Policy Center) are just a few of the predictions the experts were making that year:

- "Civilization will end within 15 or 30 years unless immediate action is taken against problems facing mankind." —Biologist George Wald, Harvard University, April 19, 1970

- By 1995, "somewhere between 75 and 85 percent of all the species of living animals will be extinct." —Senator Gaylord Nelson, quoting Dr. S. Dillon Ripley, *Look* magazine, April 1970

- Because of increased dust, cloud cover, and water vapor, "the planet will cool, the water vapor will fall and freeze, and a new Ice Age will be born." —*Newsweek* magazine, January 26, 1970

- The world will be "eleven degrees colder in the year 2000. This is about twice what it would take to put us into an ice age." —Ecologist Kenneth Watt, speaking at Swarthmore University, April 19, 1970

- "We are in an environmental crisis which threatens the survival of this nation, and of the world as a suitable place of human habitation." —Biologist Barry Commoner, University of Washington, writing in the journal *Environment*, April 1970

- "Man must stop pollution and conserve his resources, not merely to enhance existence but to save the race from the intolerable deteriorations and possible extinction." —*New York Times* editorial, April 20, 1970

- "By 1985, air pollution will have reduced the amount of sunlight reaching earth by one half." —*Life* magazine, January 1970

- "Population will inevitably and completely outstrip whatever small increases in food supplies we make." —Biologist Paul Ehrlich, interview in *Mademoiselle* magazine, April 1970

- "Air pollution … is certainly going to take hundreds of thousands of lives in the next few years alone." —Paul Ehrlich, interview in *Mademoiselle* magazine, April 1970

- Ehrlich also predicted that in 1973, 200,000 Americans would die from air pollution, and that by 1980, the life expectancy of Americans would be forty-two years.

- "It is already too late to avoid mass starvation." —Earth Day organizer Denis Hayes, *The Living Wilderness*, Spring 1970

- "By the year 2000 … the entire world, with the exception of Western Europe, North America and Australia, will be in famine." —Professor Peter Gunter, North Texas State University, *The Living Wilderness*, Spring 1970

Luckily none of this bad stuff happened. So, it must mean that Earth Day worked. Hurrah for Earth Day, savior of the planet!

E

EASTER ISLAND

Dread warning from history as to the terrible fate which awaits us because of our wanton selfishness, greed, and refusal to live more sustainably … apparently.

"I have often asked myself, 'What did the Easter Islander who cut down the last palm tree say while he was doing it?' Like modern loggers, did he shout 'Jobs, not trees!'? Or: 'Technology will solve our problems, never fear, we'll find a substitute for wood'? —Jared Diamond, *Collapse: How Societies Choose to Fail or Succeed*

Hmm. I think Diamond is trying to make a sociopolitical point there. But he has expressed it so subtly it's hard to do justice to the nuance, sophistication, and intellectual richness of his argument. Still, I shall have a go: "WESTERN INDUSTRIAL CIVILIZATION IS COMMITTING ECOCIDE JUST LIKE EASTER ISLAND DID. CAPITALISM IS WRONG, JULIAN SIMON IS A LIAR AND YOU'RE ALL GOING TO DIE, LOSER FOOLS!!!"

Except there are a couple of things wrong with Jared Diamond's fashionably doomy thesis. The first and most obvious one is that the world is not like an incredibly remote and isolated small island in the South Pacific. It's much bigger. It's less densely populous than Easter Island was at its peak. It comprises a large number of mature sovereign states, where property rights and a market price mechanism give people a strong disincentive to chop down all the trees and build lots of pointless statues, or whatever Diamond thinks happens in his fantasy evil capitalist system. Easter Island isn't a microcosm, a "metaphor" as Diamond puts it. It's an anomaly.

And the second is that, historically, his thesis is bunkum. According to Diamond's version—possibly based on Dr. Seuss's *The Lorax*—the Easter Island civilization collapsed in war and cannibalism and starvation because the islanders became so obsessed with building their huge stone statues that they cut down all the trees needed to move them around. This, in turn, meant they could no longer build fishing boats to feed themselves.

What carbon dating, the archaeological record, and the vast bulk of serious research into the subject show is that, far from inviting their own destruction, the hapless Easter Islanders were killed off by slavers, smallpox, and syphilis. This is why they stopped building the statues. As for those chopped-down trees, while they were certainly a loss, they were not essential to the nutrition or survival of the islanders who survived happily on intensive farming and fish. Until they got wiped out, that is.

Ecocide

Imaginary crime which environmental activists—notably one Polly Higgins, "international environmental lawyer"—are trying determinedly to put onto the UN's statute books, having taken Jared Diamond far too seriously.

[BAT-SPLATTING, BIRD-SLICING] ECO-CRUCIFIXES (*See* BATS; WIND FARMS)

ECO-FASCISM

Fascism? Really? Isn't that a bit harsh, a bit demeaning, a bit reductive of all those caring, well-meaning environmentalists out there who just want to make the world a better place?

Clearly, you have much to learn about how the green movement rolls.

Here's Jonah Goldberg's definition from his highly readable *Liberal Fascism*:

"Fascism is a religion of the state. It assumes the organic unity of the body politic and longs for a national leader attuned to the will of the people. It is totalitarian in that it views everything as political and holds that any action by the state is justified to achieve the common good. It takes responsibility for all aspects of life, including our health and well-being, and seeks to impose uniformity of thought and action, whether by force or through regulation and social pressure. Everything, including the economy and religion, must be aligned with its objectives. Any rival identity is part of the 'problem' and therefore defined as the enemy."

E

Pretty much everything in that description accords with everything you'll read about environmentalist philosophy (and action) elsewhere in this book. The only differences are that Eco-Fascism is not nationalistic but supra-nationalistic—that is, its ultimate aims are towards a One World Government; and that, inevitably as a consequence of this, there is no single leader you could cite as the movement's figurehead.

But if you had to, I'd probably go for either Maurice Strong (q.v.) or George Soros (q.v.).

ECOLOGY

Before ecologists there were naturalists—a species which is now almost extinct. Naturalists looked at nature and saw that it was good. They traveled to exotic places, risking malaria, shipwreck, and mass seduction by Tahitian nubiles, to illustrate and harvest the plant and animal samples which would later form the basis of

the world's great museum collections. Then they wrote illuminating texts based on their hard-won expertise—books which completely transformed the way we look at the natural world, such Charles Darwin's *On the Origin of Species*.

But that was then. Today, instead of naturalists and biologists and zoologists and ornithologists and herpetologists, we have a new breed of scientists who see their purpose as being not so much to celebrate the natural world as to denigrate man's influence on it.

Welcome to the misanthropic world of ecology—not so much a hard science as a bastard hybrid of cod-sociology and secular religion.

Part of its problem is its highly unscientific practice of rejecting empiricism in favor of grand universal doom theories. Built into ecology is the notion that the natural world is in dire crisis and urgently in need of defense by—who else?—ecologists. In places, they may have a point. What undermines their case is that in order to make it they are far too eager to use scaremongering "projections" and manipulated evidence rather than solid real-world data.

But the real problem with ecology is that it has lent spurious scientific respectability to the modern environmental movement's instinctive misanthropy and anti-capitalism. If you believe—as ecology does—that *Homo sapiens* is but one species among many, no better or worse than mollusks or bacteria, then it ceases to be a problem when you take away his freedoms and trample on his efforts for a better life: after all, you're doing it for the greater cause—the good of the planet.

One of the first to notice the way ecological theory had trickled into mainstream thought was Julian Simon. "Ecology teaches us that humankind is not the centre of the planet. Ecology has taught us that the whole earth is part of our 'body' and that we must learn to respect it as we respect life—the whales, the seals, the forests, the seas."

This shift, he noticed, could be detected in the changing nature of scientific textbooks. In the old days, "the descriptions of many birds included evaluations of their effects on humanity in general and on farmers in particular; a bird that helped agriculture was more highly valued than a bird which harmed it." But in newer books, this centuries-old acceptance that the earth is man's domain had given a new strain of politically correct self-hatred and eco-guilt. Suddenly, mankind was being assessed—and held to account—for its "effect upon the birds rather than vice versa."

Ecology, you could argue, has replaced Christianity as the West's dominant religious philosophy. The Bible urged the human species "be fruitful and multiply" with man given dominion over nature. As far as the new Green Bible is concerned, however, human beings are a nature's problem and need to be bludgeoned into submission by Gaia-defending ecologists.

ECO-NAZIS (*See* GODWIN'S LAW)

ELECTRIC CARS

Zero emissions? Yeah, right. Even before it rolls off the production line, an electric car has created more than twice as many carbon dioxide emissions as a conventional car. (Electric: 30,000 pounds of CO_2 emissions; conventional: 14,000 pounds.) That's because the manufacturing process—notably the energy used to create its battery and to mine the lithium—is so eco-unfriendly.

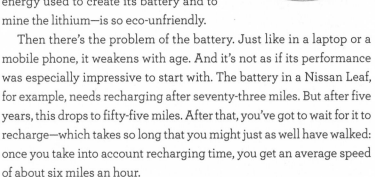

Then there's the problem of the battery. Just like in a laptop or a mobile phone, it weakens with age. And it's not as if its performance was especially impressive to start with. The battery in a Nissan Leaf, for example, needs recharging after seventy-three miles. But after five years, this drops to fifty-five miles. After that, you've got to wait for it to recharge—which takes so long that you might just as well have walked: once you take into account recharging time, you get an average speed of about six miles an hour.

Over its entire lifetime, Bjorn Lomborg noted in the *Wall Street Journal*, an electric car may be responsible for 8.7 tons of CO_2 less than the average conventional car. This might sound impressive, but the market price for that amount of CO_2 (on the European emissions trading market; the U.S. one collapsed) is about $50.

Yet the U.S. government subsidizes electric car-buyers with up to $7,500. And—as Lomborg noted—that's not counting the $5.5 billion in federal grants and loans that go directly to battery and electric car makers like California's Fisker Automotive and Tesla Motors.

Isn't green crony capitalism a wonderful thing?

ELEPHANT IN THE ROOM (*See* OVERPOPULATION)

ENVIRONMENT CORRESPONDENTS

One of the purposes, traditionally, of the journalistic specialist is to differentiate between the truth and the BS spewed out by publicists, official spokesmen, and lobbyists. Through a combination of expert knowledge, industry contacts, and an eye for a good story, the specialist gives readers/listeners/viewers an insider's deep understanding of the reality behind the lies and spin, a sense of what's really going on.

Unless, of course, they are an environment correspondent, in which case the opposite is true.

An environment correspondent's job entails:

- Transcribing press releases from the Intergovernmental Panel on Climate Change, Al Gore, the Sierra Club, Greenpeace, the EPA, the World Wildlife Fund, etc.

- Giving the story an urgent, scary headline so that readers/viewers/listeners are sufficiently overwhelmed with fear, panic, and breast-beating eco-guilt not to start asking awkward questions like, "Hey, didn't we hear something similar last week? And the week before?? And the week before that???"

- Flying to Rio/Copenhagen/Cancun/Bali/Doha and similar agreeable destinations two or three times a year in order to big up the latest UN climate/biodiversity/sustainability conference and make it sound like it wasn't a complete waste of time.

- Earning a bit of extra money on the side being paid to host panel discussions at faux-academic conferences in which climate scientists, environmentalists, and green activists all agree that the global eco-crisis is worsening by the day and that the only solution is for more government money to be spent on research and further conferences in which climate scientists, environmentalists, and green activists can meet to review how grave the crisis is and how much more government money needs to be spent on it.

- Kind of feeling good about what they're doing because they only studied for a humanities degree at college, but this stuff they're writing about now, it's quite technical and complex and science-y, and it means hanging out with impressive people who've got actual Ph.D.s while simultaneously saving the world. Beats straight news reporting, that's for sure.

- Writing a light-hearted column called "Eco-Worrier" to show that being green isn't just about serious stuff like waking up with night sweats, shivering in terror about the future of the polar bear, but also about really hilarious stuff like accidentally putting a cereal packet in the compost bin which was meant for plastics.

ENVIRONMENTAL PROTECTION AGENCY (EPA)

Communist sleeper cell introduced to heart of the U.S. government system by Richard Nixon in the mistaken belief that paying Danegeld to your enemies will make them leave you alone.

Since 1970, the EPA has swollen to embrace 17,000 employees, many, if not most of them, deep-green ideologues on a holy mission to rein in

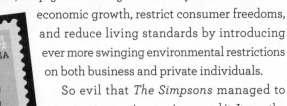

economic growth, restrict consumer freedoms, and reduce living standards by introducing ever more swinging environmental restrictions on both business and private individuals.

So evil that *The Simpsons* managed to construct an entire movie around it. It was the EPA, of course, in *The Simpsons Movie*, which decides that the appropriate punishment for

Springfield's breach of environmental regulations is to seal the entire town in a giant glass dome—and then kill all the occupants.

As Homer would say: "It's funny because it's true."

ETHANOL (*See also* BIOFUELS)

Heavily subsidized and now entirely pointless U.S. mandate whereby farmers are paid to turn their food crops to fuel—supposedly to reduce dependency on oil imports and to reduce carbon emissions.

The latest research suggests that, far from reducing CO_2 emissions, biofuels increase them. Nor does the energy security argument wash: thanks to its shale fields, the United States is becoming less and less dependent on imported oil.

What ethanol does do very successfully though is drive up food and fuel prices, ensure that cars run fewer miles to the gallon, increase water consumption, and help encourage starvation and food riots in the developing world. Very eco-friendly!

Everyone Is Entitled to His Own Opinion but Not His Own Facts

Environmentalists/Warmists frequently deploy this line in an attempt to silence their critics and dismiss contrarian evidence. The Yiddish name for this grotesque inversion of reality is "chutzpah." The psychological term is "projection."

E

EXTINCTION RATE

The fire-breathing crevice ant; Clinton's throat gargler; the Treble-finned lunar shark; Obama's testicular mite; the Swumple; the Mendacious Algora; Crocker's Imperial gecko; the gray, horrible, devil fungus; the Cromblewomble....

Go on, you can join in, too. It's a fun game that everyone in the family can play, from one to 101. All you have to do is make an endless list of all the imaginary species that you think might have gone extinct this year—and, hey, presto! You're just like a real-life conservation biologist.

Just how many species are we losing each year? If you believe Harvard biologist E. O. Wilson, it's 27,000 a year. According to British conservationist Norman Myers, it's as many as 40,000. But whatever the precise figure, it's got to be serious, right? I mean, those experts, they wouldn't just be plucking these numbers from the top of their head....

Actually, they would. Myers's figure wasn't even an estimate—just an assumption. In 1979, he wrote: "Let us suppose that, as a consequence of this man-handling of natural environments, the final one quarter of this century witnesses the elimination of one million species—a far from unlikely prospect. This would work out, during the course of 25 years, at an average extinction rate of 40,000 species per year."

What's missing from these projections—(hmm ... why does this sound so familiar?)—is hard evidence.

Wilson's figure is based on a theory called a species-area curve, which predicts that as habitats diminish so a proportionate number of species will be driven to extinction. But as the scholar Willis Eschenbach has noted, this just doesn't accord with real-world data. We can tell this from the extinction rate among birds and mammals. If Wilson's theory is correct, then we should be expecting to lose, *every year*, pro rata, around sixteen continental bird species and eleven continental mammal species. In reality, however, in the last *500 years* a grand total of just six continental bird and three mammal species have gone extinct.

The figure for island species loss—as opposed to continental species loss—is slightly higher because island populations are more vulnerable to problems like alien predator species, such as rats, and also to being hunted to death like the Dodo. Even then, the total of all mammals and birds lost in the last 500 years is dramatically smaller than Wilson's projections, let alone Myers's "assumption" would suggest: sixty-one mammals and 129 birds.

Does this mean we should not regret the passing of the bluebuck (hunted to death by European settlers in about 1800), the Labrador Duck (shot and trapped to extinction in around 1878), the Omilteme cottontail rabbit (reason for extinction unknown), and the rest? Of course not. The world would undoubtedly be a richer place were we still able to see Dodos and Great Auks waddling around their natural habitats.

What it does mean, however, is that next time we hear an environmental campaign group trotting out the figure that up to 1,000 species are being lost each day, or that humans are causing a "sixth mass extinction" to rival the asteroid that killed the dinosaurs, we should probably reach for our Brownings rather than our checkbooks.

FAITH

Modern environmentalism is only comprehensible in terms of faith. It is a form of antinomianism—that is, it depends for existence on a series of accepted "truths" which brook no argument and are entirely immune to logic or rational criticism. To be a true believer in the environmentalist creed, first you must suspend all doubt.

Here are the key articles of the green faith.

- Humans are a cancer on the earth.

- But future generations are so special that massive sacrifices must be made in the present in order to satisfy the golden, blessed ones' future needs.

- Resources—especially fossil fuels—are so scarce that they must be rationed (see Peak Oil).

- Renewables are the solution. Even when they're obviously not.

- Economic growth—Western civilization generally—is bad because it entails increased consumption, which uses up scarce resources.

- Left to their own devices—as you'd expect from people who are a cancer on the earth—humans cannot be trusted to do the right thing and must therefore have their freedoms stripped and their ways of life regulated by an enlightened ruling class of "experts."

- Before man arrived, nature was a pristine Eden of untrammeled loveliness. We must do everything in our power to restore the world to its prelapsarian state of perfection (see Rewilding)—regardless of the economic or human cost.

- Earth justice requires that resources are distributed evenly. Therefore, it is only proper that transnational bodies such as the UN should oversee sustainability programs which not only safeguard the environment, but which also transfer money—by compulsion, if necessary—from rich to poor, men to women, present generations to future ones....

- Believers in the green faith serve a higher cause than objective truth. It is therefore entirely forgivable if, in the service of this higher cause, they twist the evidence to suit their particular ends.

- It's All Our Fault. Everything. Always.

FEEDBACKS

Boring but important, this. Most scientists agree—alarmists and skeptics alike—that a doubling of atmospheric CO_2 levels will result in a temperature rise of around 1.1 degrees Celsius.

If this doesn't sound like very much, you're right: it isn't.

1.1 degrees Celsius is less than the temperature change you experience between breakfast and lunch, between New York and D.C., between standing at the bottom of a hill and climbing, say, 1,000 feet to the top.

So, why are the alarmists urging us to bomb the global economy back to the Dark Ages in order to deal with a menace about ten times less threatening than a weekend's skiing in Vail?

Because they believe in these things called "positive feedbacks"— additional effects such as thinning cloud cover and methane released from the tundra by melting permafrost, which supposedly amplify mild warming into dangerous warming.

Climate realists such as Professor Richard Lindzen and Dr. Roy Spencer argue otherwise: that far from being "positive" these feedbacks are either neutral or "negative," due to balancing effects such as increased cloud cover.

F

Of course, eminent though these realists may be in their fields, they could still be wrong (*see* "appeal to authority," p. 118). But so far, the real world evidence appears to support them—and not the alarmists' computer models.

Here is how Dr. Lindzen puts it:

- In the last 150 years there has been a doubling of atmospheric CO_2.

- In the same period there has been a warming of about 0.8 degrees.

The warming effect of the doubled CO_2 in that period ought to have been at least 1 degree Celsius. But the actual warming has been 0.2 degrees less than that.

Therefore, the logical conclusion is that climate sensitivity has been overestimated in the alarmists' models. The theories simply don't accord with the real world data.

"FEEDING THE MASSES ON UNICORN RIBS"—HAT TIP TO WALTER RUSSELL MEAD (*See* GREEN JOBS)

Fisker Karma

Green plutocrat's vanity toy subsidized by the U.S. taxpayer. In 2010, the Department of Energy awarded Fisker—a Finnish car manufacturer—a $529 million green energy loan to ease its transition into the U.S. market.

And what did American taxpayers get in return for their largesse? A $107,000 car which broke down on its first test drive with less than 200 miles on its odometer. Several incidents in which Fiskers mysteriously caught fire. Numerous product recalls due to faulty battery packs, leaking coolant, and improperly positioned hose clamps.

Bad karma, man.

F

FOLLOW THE MONEY

One of the many perks of being a climate skeptic—that and our all-expenses-paid annual climate deniers' polar-bear hunting expedition to Nunavat every year, financed by the Koch Brothers—is the vast salary we receive, courtesy of Big Oil, Big Coal, and Big Evil.

This book, for example, was dictated—between cocktails—to my manservant as I lounged on my third and favorite sundeck on my 500-foot private yacht *ManBearPig*. Obviously, I'd never write the nonsense I write about climate change and the environment if it weren't for the money. I lie because I am paid to lie.

I wish.

Between 1989 and 2010, the U.S. government alone spent $79 billion on climate change research and technology. According to blogger and author Jo Nova, this was 3,500 times the amount made available to those scientists who were climate skeptics.

In the same period, the European Union spent well over $100 billion on climate funding. As blogger and author Richard North has noted, this means that, in terms of equivalent funding, "combating climate change" has proved five times more costly than the previous most expensive scientific experiment in history, the Manhattan Project to build the nuclear bomb.

On top of that is the funding from environmental advocacy organizations: in the United States alone, there are 26,540 of them with annual spending budget, estimated by author and investigative journalist Elizabeth Nickson, of $9 billion a year.

During the Fakegate, er, Climategate (q.v.) "scandal" we were invited by environmental activist Peter Gleick to be shocked by the fact that the climate-skeptical Heartland Institute is funded to the tune of $4.7 million a year. Only a small proportion of that budget is spent on climate skepticism (mainly its annual climate conference; and modest stipends for in-house experts).

Now, compare the minuscule amount spent on skeptics by Heartland to the truckloads of cash handed to the climate alarmists by green NGOs such as the Sierra Club (budget: $80 million), the World Wildlife Fund (budget in excess of $100 million) or the environmental advocacy group Climateworks which receives $166 million a year from just two charitable foundations (the Hewlett Foundation and the Packard Foundation) for its work spreading green propaganda.

Still wonder why so many people "believe" in the threat of climate change? Upton Sinclair knew the answer years ago:

"It is difficult to get a man to understand something when his salary depends on his not understanding it."

FOOD MILES (*See also* OUT OF SEASON)

Guilt myth devised by bleeding hearts to make you feel bad when you eat asparagus grown in Chile or strawberries from Egypt, and to make them feel good when they munch sanctimoniously on a turnip whose main recommendation is that it was grown one hundred yards down the road—and is therefore virtuous because so little energy was expended bringing it to their plate.

Except it's often just not true. As blogger Stephen Budiansky—"The Liberal Curmudgeon"—has shown, once you take into account total energy costs of food, not just transport (a relatively minor part of the equation), but factors like fertilizer and artificial heat, it often works out more environmentally friendly to eat stuff grown abroad (yes, even if it's flown in by airplane!) than from your bijou, doorstep organic food market.

A zillion times cheaper, too.

FORESTRY

Oh those truffula trees....

I blame Dr. Seuss's *The Lorax*; and Tolkien's Ents; and that shiny, magical, healing tree nexus thingamajig in *Dances with Smurfs* (a.k.a. *Avatar*); and all those other anthropomorphized bits of animated twiggery which have helped contribute to this credulous notion so many people seem to have these days that trees are just like us: only better....

Look, I like a nice tree, too: oak, for personal preference, being as I'm an Englishman. I like climbing trees; I like walking through woodland; I like California Redwoods and Louisianan live oaks and Australian gum trees and the pines near the Linn of Quoich in Deeside and the Flame Trees of Thika (wherever Thika is, but I'm sure I'd love the Flame Trees there if I saw them because how could I not?).

But what I don't do because I'm not a greenie and I'm not insane (for the visual definition of both, google "tree-hugging hippies" and try to track down—if they haven't deleted it—the footage of Gaia-lovers tearfully embracing trees and begging their forgiveness for man's crimes against them) is confuse them with human beings.

For example, no tree is worth the eye—let alone the life—of a forestry worker injured by a chunk of metal placed in the trunk by some well-meaning eco-activist. But I quite understand why eco-activists do such things: in large part because they have been brainwashed and—like many in the green movement—have no real understanding about what it is that forestry entails.

F

As ever, the green NGOs have a lot to answer for here. In 1996, the World Wildlife Fund garnered headlines worldwide thanks to its ludicrous claim that the world was losing fifty million species a year—and that the majority of these were victims of the commercial logging industry.

Logging, by the way, rather than forestry or silviculture is what you call it if you're an eco-activist. It conjures up instant images of nasty men in hard hats clambering all over the Amazon and the Pacific Northwest and Malaysia, cackling gleefully as—whoops—there goes another baby orangutan, but hey, who cares, because it will make a nice piece of teak garden furniture for some bloated plutocrat who probably works in the oil industry.

Many of the green NGOs are in on the act: the Sierra Club is calling for "zero cut" and an end to commercial forestry on federal public lands in the United States; the Rainforest Action Network is demanding a 75 percent reduction in wood use in North America by 2015; Greenpeace is lobbying the United Nations Inter-Governmental Panel on Forests to demand countries reduce their wood use and to adopt "environmentally-friendly substitutes instead." (What those substitutes might be, Greenpeace mysteriously doesn't specify....)

There are at least three problems here. The first is that every year, we humans consume around 3.4 billion cubic meters of wood—and it's got to come from somewhere, most likely these things we call "trees."

Second, silviculture is in fact one of the most eco-friendly industries in the world. It's renewable and sustainable (foresters only reap what they have first planted, thus ensuring there is no need to encroach on old growth woodland); and whether used for fuel, buildings, furniture, or paper, wood is less harmful than the nearest substitute.

Third, like so many of the green movement's great ideas, this campaign against forestry achieves the exact opposite of what it's supposed to do. Most forests *need* active management. Without humans to clear the underbrush and thin out the trees, they grow spindly and are more susceptible to devastating fire. But when managed—when humans have an economic stake in them—they don't just stay healthier, but they actually expand, as is happening in India and China where demand for wood by the burgeoning middle class means the areas of land under forestation are actually increasing.

But I guess if you believe that Treebeard is a real character, that foresters don't deserve a living, and that timber products are almost as bad as dead baby seals, then such sophisticated arguments probably aren't going to penetrate your wooden head.

Forestry Stewardship Council (FSC)

Greenie NGOs operate a bit like the mafia: you wanna do business then you gotta pay protection money. The FSC is an example of this. It sounds neutral and independent, but in fact it was partly created by Greenpeace and the World Wildlife Fund in order to exert control over the forestry industry. There are plenty of other equally rigorous forest certification standard-setters around the world—but only one that gets the greenies' bully boy activists off your back.

FRIENDLY LAWSUITS

Green NGOs and government environmental agencies work like tag teams: Greenpeace and Friends of the Earth go hand in hand with the Department of Energy and Climate Change; the Environmental Protection Agency plays Mr. Nice (well, relatively nice) to the Environmental Defense Fund's Mr. Nasty. They're often staffed by exactly the same kind of people, with exactly the same violently anti-capitalist aims. The only difference is that the state employees have to be a bit more discreet about it.

Here's how one of their favorite scams works: the "friendly lawsuit." Suppose, for example, some bright spark at the EPA has dreamed up yet another brilliant enviro-fascistic scheme to destroy industry. A new regulation, maybe, to force coal-fired plants to install haze-reducing, pollution-control equipment at a cost of $1.5 billion. Well, of course, there might be a few complaints from the evil coal industry.

In order to bypass potential legal resistance, the EPA puts on its innocent face and deploys the time-honored playground excuse: "bad boys made me do it." It does this by quietly asking its friends at the Environmental Defense Fund to file a lawsuit against the EPA, demanding that the EPA introduce the very same legislation that the EPA wanted anyway.

When the coal industry complains that jobs are being killed, prices inflated, and margins reduced by new regulations which nobody save a few hard-left activists wanted or needed, the EPA replies that it had no choice: it acted in order to settle a lawsuit by environmental groups.

In any other criminal business—such as arranging deliberate motor crashes in order to make false claims for whiplash injuries—this would qualify as fraud and a conviction would result in jail sentences. Apparently, though, where the environment industry is concerned, such moral and legal niceties need not apply.

FUKUSHIMA

How many people died as a result of radioactive leaks in the great Fukushima nuclear disaster of 2011? The same number who died in the similarly legendary nuclear disaster at Three Mile Island, of course.

Zero.

How many people are going to die as a result of radioactive exposure from the great Fukushima nuclear disaster? Probably on the order of zero.

How many people are going to be born with genetic mutations or other problems as a result of Fukushima? Zero.

And how many people lost their lives as a result of the earthquake and tsunami, which led to the breach in the Fukushima nuclear power plant? Around 20,000.

Does anyone notice the discrepancy here? Nobody was seriously harmed by the radioactive leak at Fukushima. Many thousands were

killed, injured, orphaned, widowed, or rendered homeless by the earthquake and tsunami. Yet where did the world's media concentrate the brunt of its attention? On the complete non-story of the nuclear disaster that never was.

"Japan nuke disaster. PANIC! Workers halt desperate struggle to stop meltdown. 140,000 warned to stay indoors. Anti-nuke pills sell out on jittery U.S. West Coast," reported the *New York Daily News*.

So great was the global hysteria that in Germany, following nationwide protests, the Merkel government agreed to phase out nuclear power altogether. The result? Massive increases in the cost of energy (Germany's transition to renewables will cost it an estimated one trillion euros, $1.3 trillion, by the end of the 2030s). And a similarly massive increase in the use of coal-fired power, which causes notably more damage to the environment and public health than has ever been caused by the nuclear industry.

FUTURE GENERATIONS 1

Imaginary children of the future endlessly invoked by environmental campaigners, junk economists (see Stern, Nicholas), and vote-grubbing politicians in order to justify the suffering caused to present generations by their disastrous and expensive climate policies.

Because they are imaginary and non-existent, we can but speculate what they are like. But the way Al Gore and Company go on about them, I expect they must be something really, extra special. Probably, they all have kindly, beautiful faces and gentle natures and sublime intellects, are fluent in at least two dozen languages, capable of solving a Rubik's cube in under ten seconds, versatile in all manner of vegetarian cuisine (especially their to-die-for meat-free moussaka), with scratch golf handicaps, and great senses of humor, but who dedicate most of their perfect lives to healing the sick and creating world peace.

Don't you feel so much better now, that in the name of these people, all you're being asked to sacrifice is your job, your kids' jobs, your savings, your freedoms, your standard of living, your national sovereignty?

Future Generations 2

"Future generations will wonder in bemused amazement that the early 21st century's developed world went into hysterical panic over a globally averaged temperature increase of a few tenths of a degree, and, on the basis of gross exaggerations of highly uncertain computer projections combined into implausible chains of inference, proceeded to contemplate a roll-back of the industrial age."
—Dr. Richard Lindzen, MIT

F

GAP ANALYSIS PROGRAM (GAP)

Scheme introduced under the Clinton administration to remove land from private ownership so that it can never again be used by wicked humans for dangerous activities like: job creation, economic growth, profit, hunting, fishing, camping, ornithology, naturalism, naturism, leisure, or pleasure of any kind deemed unsuitable by environmentalist brownshirts.

GASLAND
(*See* FRACKNATION INSTEAD: IT'S MUCH BETTER, MUCH MORE ACCURATE, AND IT HAS A CAMEO FROM JAMES DELINGPOLE)

Anti-fracking propaganda movie famous for the scene where a resident shows how he can set fire to the methane leaking out of his kitchen faucet. What director Josh Fox doesn't tell you—and he knew this right from the start—is that in parts of the United States, including the one featured in that scene, methane has been leaking out of faucets for years long before fracking for shale gas started. Truly, Fox is the new Michael Moore. And I'm not altogether sure that's a compliment.

GEORGIA GUIDESTONES

Bizarro eco-fascist monument erected on a hilltop in Georgia at the behest of a mysterious man calling himself Robert C. Christian, in which the environmentalist equivalent of the Ten Commandments are inscribed on slabs in eight different languages.

Commandment no. 1 says: "MAINTAIN HUMANITY UNDER 500,000,000 IN PERPETUAL BALANCE WITH NATURE."

G

Hope nobody takes these commandments seriously. If we obeyed that particular injunction, it would involve killing 6.5 billion people.

GERMANY

Former home of the world's greenest government ever (1933 to 1945), a tradition it continues to maintain with some of the most active green MPs and the strictest environmental regulation anywhere in Europe.

Thanks to its concerted drive for renewable energy—including solar panels on every church roof and ancient forests chopped down to clear the way for more wind farms—Germany has now successfully driven one fifth of its population into "fuel poverty." That's those crazy Germans for you: they don't like to do anything by halves.

GIBSON GUITARS (*See also* LACEY ACT)

American icon; canary in the coalmine for the global environmentalist war on capitalism.

In 2009 and again in 2011, when it was raided by Obama's Feds, apparently for breaching environmental laws regarding importation of tropical hardwoods. No connection, surely, with the fact that the CEO Henry E. Juszkziewicz is guilty of being both a Republican donor and an employer of non-unionized labor?

GLACIER

The glaciers are melting! The glaciers are melting!

Yes, as they have been for the last 10,000 years since we started emerging from the most recent Ice Age. But not all glaciers. In the Karokoram—the most heavily glaciated part of the world after Greenland and Antarctica, containing nearly 3 percent of the planet's total ice area, glaciers are expanding. And in the Himalayas—*see* Glaciergate—reports of the local glaciers' imminent demise has been greatly exaggerated. As, too, has the popular idea that once the glaciers melt, India's water supply will dry up. Ninety-six percent of the water in the Ganges comes from rainfall, not melting ice.

GLACIERGATE

Will the Himalayan glaciers really disappear by 2035? According to the Intergovernmental Panel on Climate Changes's 2007 Assessment Report—and who would quibble with the "gold standard" of climate research?—the likelihood was "very high."

Or was it?

On closer examination, Glaciergate turned out to be a lie based on a misrepresentation inspired by a farrago of nonsense.

It had begun life as a claim made in 1999 by a researcher called Dr. Syed Hasnain in an Indian environmental magazine called *Down to Earth* and later repeated in *New Scientist.* Somehow it then found its way into the IPCC's Fourth Assessment Report—despite the fact that one of the greatest experts in this field, Austrian glaciologist Dr. Georg Kaser, had described it as "so wrong it is not even worth dismissing."

When the claim was further ridiculed by Indian glaciologist Dr. Vijay Raina, an unlikely defender stepped forward to defend Hasnain: none other than Dr. Rajendra Pachauri, head of the IPCC. Pachauri accused Raina of "voodoo science." (Pachauri was subsequently asked to apologize by India's environment minister.)

The plot thickened still further when it emerged that Hasnain was one of Pachauri's employees—head of the Energy and Resources

Institute's new glaciology unit—and that his claim may have been instrumental in helping to secure part of a $500,000 Carnegie Corporation grant into researching melting Himalayan glaciers.

Pachauri began backtracking, blaming the erroneous claim on "human error." However, further investigation by another IPCC author, Professor Murari Lal, concluded that it was not a mistake. The clear implication is that a known untruth had deliberately been inserted into the IPCC report for reasons we can only guess at—but which surely had nothing to do with the IPCC's director's appetite for that generous grant funding.

Gleick, Peter

Berkeley Ph.D.; MacArthur Genius award winner; member of the National Academy of Sciences; director of Pacific Institute; scourge of climate skeptics; launch chairman of American Geophysical Union task force on "scientific ethics and integrity"; expert witness at 2007 Senate Committee hearing on Climate Change Research and Science Integrity; very exemplar of all that is good and noble and true.

GLEICKGATE

Gleickgate was originally meant to be the greenies' answer to Climategate.

"It's a rare glimpse behind the wall of a key climate denial organization. It shows there is a co-ordinated effort to have an alternative reality on the climate science in order to have an impact on the policy," a spokesman for Greenpeace told the *Guardian*.

Wow! Sounds damning. And just what did the scandal involve?

Well, apparently, a sinister, well-funded, right-wing think tank called the Heartland Institute, with help from the wicked Koch Brothers, had been financing a campaign of denialism, which included discouraging "teachers from teaching science."

G

The left-liberal media was in no doubt that this was a very important story. Much bigger than Climategate, certainly, to judge by their coverage. But those on the other side of the debate smelled a rat. This phrase about trying to stop "teachers from teaching science," for example. It didn't sound like anything a climate realist would say, but something more like the paranoid fantasy of a deranged alarmist engaged in a desperate smear job.

Sure enough, it turned out that the most incriminating documents were faked. They had been stolen using identity theft—and then doctored—by a man named Peter Gleick (q.v.). With delicious irony, see above, Gleick prides himself on being a paragon of moral integrity and crusader for transparency and honesty in science.

Though Gleick eventually came clean and apologized for his "lapse," he refused to accept responsibility for the inept alterations. Perhaps this was out of embarrassment. One of the faked lines had the Heartland Institute supposedly plotting to stop "teachers from teaching science." As one commentator noted: "Basically, it reads like it was written from a secret villain lair in a Batman comic. By an intern."

But it all turned out nicely in the end, for Gleick at any rate. When his thieving, lying, and fraud was exposed, the left-liberal media rushed eagerly to his defense. Daily Kos hailed him a "hero scientist"; the *LA Times* noted that Gleick's actions were "directly from the denialists' playbook"—and certainly no more reprehensible than the "hack attack at the University of East Anglia"; while, according to *Scientific American*, Gleick's lie was clearly moral because his cause was just.

This a rhetorical question, I know. But these people: Do they have no shame?

GLOBAL WARMING: IS IT HAPPENING?

As a self-appointed global warming expert with at least as many climate science qualifications as Al Gore, Bill McKibben, and Ed Begley Jr., I frequently find myself being asked the question: "Are we all going to die?"

The correct answer is, of course, "Yes. Depending on time scale."

This answer is also the right response to the question about global warming. (Though "No" would be equally accurate. As would: "Kind of." As would: "What kind of a damn fool question is that?")

It sounds evasive but is in fact the only honest response to the global warming debate. If you were to take 1850 as your starting point, then yes, since then we have experienced about 0.8 degrees Celsius of "global warming." You'd get about the same figure if you took 1979 as your base year and made 1998 your end date. "0.8 degrees in just ten over years! So, that's the equivalent of nearly 8 degrees in a century!! We're all going to fry!!!" you could tell your more catastrophically minded friends. And with that hard temperature data to back up your claims, how could they possibly doubt you?

Then again, you could go the other way, too. For example, if you took 1997 as your starting point, you would find that there has been no statistically significant warming since. Or, if you used a 1,000-year time scale, you'd find that the world's temperatures had been gently cooling (by about 4 degrees Celsius) since their high point in the Medieval Warming Period. You'd get an even more marked cooling trend if you took as your starting point the peak of the Lower Holocene Optimum period around 8,000 years ago.

In short: global warming is happening; it isn't happening; and it really doesn't matter either way because nothing that climate has been doing in our lifetime is in any way more dramatic or weird than anything it has been doing in the last 10,000 or so years.

G

GODWIN'S LAW (*See also* NAZIS: HOW GREEN WERE THEY?)

Now familiar adage—"As an online discussion grows longer, the probability of a comparison involving Nazis or Hitler approaches"—that should be ignored.

Eco-Nazis is a term we should use interchangeably with Eco-Fascists a) because they hate it, b) because it's true, and c) because Godwin's Law sucks.

Not only is Godwin's Law an affront to humor (how could P. J. O'Rourke have written his classic 1982 essay on Safety Nazis if there'd some imaginary censor hovering at his shoulder, tut-tutting about the impropriety of the joke?), but it's also an assault on the rich metaphorical possibilities of the English language. Being unfunny and limiting freedom of speech: isn't that ever so slightly—um—Nazi-ish?

Look, let's get real here. There's an excellent reason why the Second World War, and the Nazis most especially, are so frequently mined for metaphor and allusion. It's because it's within living memory, it's because everyone knows something about it, and because every possible human experience is contained with it, often on the most intense and vivid level imaginable.

Of course, if someone is really bad, you're going to liken them to Hitler, Goebbels, Goering, or Himmler! (Or Stalin or Tojo, if you're feeling imaginative.) Of course, if you're talking metaphorical battles, the ones you're going to invoke are Stalingrad, El Alamein, and the Bulge. Of course you're going to describe the enemy's last defenses as his Siegfried Line, his last redoubt as his Eagle's Nest, his most vicious assaults as a blitzkrieg.

To all those greenies and lefties and greenie-lefties who find Nazi analogies discomforting I say this: if you don't like being compared to Nazis, stop behaving like Nazis. Stop your assault on property rights; stop your fascist-corporatist assault on free markets and free speech; stop killing innocents with your bans on DDT, and your state-enforced fuel poverty, and your replacement of farmland with biofuel plantations. Then you'll have no need of your precious Godwin's Law, will you?

G

GOLDEN EAGLES

Pesky avian intruder with a dangerous habit of trashing the blades of innocent wind turbines, especially in the Altamont Pass area in California. In the last twenty-five years, 2,900 golden eagles are estimated to have been killed there. We can only say "estimated" because the poor wind turbine operators are so traumatized by this vicious, unprovoked assault on their property that they cannot bring themselves to allow inspectors to collect the eagles' corpses.

GOLDEN RICE

In 2000, scientists used biotechnology to develop golden rice, a miracle strain containing enough beta carotene to prevent the one million of the world's poor who subsist mainly on rice from going blind or dying from vitamin A deficiency. But environmentalist campaigners like Greenpeace don't approve of it because it is genetically modified and—as we all know—GM is a Bad Thing. Thanks to these environmentalists' concerted opposition and noisy campaigning, golden rice still hasn't been released on the open market— despite having passed every conceivable safety test. Still, you can't save Mother Gaia without keeping a million or so innocents in pain and misery, right? And it's not like they're people Greenpeace's activists have ever met, is it? Hell, not one of them has ever once been glimpsed shopping in Whole Foods, let alone drives a Prius.

G

GOOGLE

"Don't be evil" runs Google's unofficial motto. But what could be more evil than using your vast power and resources to try and shut down free speech and force through expensive, authoritarian, anti-democratic government policy in order to deal with a non-existent problem?

Of course, that's not quite how Google saw it when in March 2011 it named its twenty-one Google science communication fellows, chosen to communicate "the science on climate change."

Here's a sample of the kind of expertise these communicators will be bringing to the debate: "We don't know everything about the climate from a scientific standpoint and there are uncertainties, but they are uncertainties over whether climate change is going to either be bad or really, really bad." —Andrew Dessler; Google fellow; climate scientist at Texas A&M University

And how many of the twenty-one fellows on that list are engaged in research on the skeptical side of the argument?

Try: zilch.

But what else do you expect of an organization whose board of directors includes one Al Gore and which is now heavily invested in renewable energy?

GORE, AL (*See also* ALGORE)

Inventor of the internet; billionaire carbon trader; Jabba the Hutt impersonator; massage enthusiast; failed former divinity student turned pagan divinity himself— Algorus, the god of hot air—CEO of the cult of Global Warming

GRAVY TRAIN
(*See* GORE, AL; HANSEN, JAMES; PACHAURI, RAJENDRA)

GREAT BRITAIN

Formerly: birthplace of Chaucer, Shakespeare, Milton, Bacon, Newton, Wren, Adam Smith, George Washington, Brunel, Darwin, etc.; inventor of cricket, parliamentary democracy, the full English breakfast, the Industrial Revolution, the internet, and the USA; proud creator of the world's greatest ever empire; famed for its magnificent, unspoilt countryside.

Currently: the only nation anywhere on Earth legally bound to commit economic suicide in the name of environmentalism. Thanks to the 2008 Climate Act, Britain is required to spend in excess of £18 billion per annum "decarbonising" the UK economy—a process which, of course, includes trashing the aforementioned magnificent, unspoilt countryside with solar panels and wind farms and crippling British business with punitive eco-taxes and regulations. If the Climate Act continues its merry path of destruction, Great Britain will eventually change its name to Grey Bogland and, in an act of hara-kiri, sink into the sea for the sake of Gaia.

Great Shift

In much the same way millenarian religious cults yearn for the apocalyptic moment when they are either assumed into heaven or sucked from the bare mountain top by the tractor beam into the belly of the alien spaceship, so greenies yearn for the Great Shift (also known as "The Transition").

This is the occasion when Western industrial civilization finally sees the errors of its ways and dismantles itself. A new age of peace and enlightenment will begin. Everyone will wear floaty, white raiment and live sustainably in small agrarian communities powered by wind turbines and the flatulent emanations of a people fed on wholesome, natural, eco-friendly flageolet beans, lentils, and Jerusalem artichokes.

G

GREEN JOBS (*See also* CHECK IN THE MAIL; SANTA CLAUS; SOROS, GEORGE)

Q. When is a job not a job?

A. When it's a *green* job.

A green job—or "green" "job," as it is more correctly written—bears much the same relationship to a real job as antimatter does to matter.

A job: creates employment; provides useful goods or services; helps satisfy consumer demand; reduces the welfare bill; expands the economy; benefits the nation; pays for itself.

A green job: does none of the above.

If you doubt this, just look at Spain, one of the first economies fully to embrace "renewable" energy such as wind power and solar power—with the result that its youth unemployment stands at more than 50 percent.

Research by Professor Gabriel Calzada Alvarez of Rey Carlos University in Madrid confirmed this. He showed that in Spain for every "green job" created by government "investment," 2.2 jobs had been killed in the real economy. A study in Britain by Verso Economics came to an even more damning conclusion: that for each green job "created" by government, 3.7 real jobs were destroyed.

In 2012, estimates from the U.S. National Renewable Energy Laboratory, an adjunct of the Department of Energy, showed that in return for spending of $9 billion the government had created just 910 new long term jobs. That works out at $9.8 million per job created. Your tax dollars at work!

GREENLAND

Was it called Greenland:

a) because when it was colonized by Vikings during the Medieval Warm Period it was considerably more verdant and fertile than the inhospitable, largely uninhabitable frozen wasteland it is today?

b) or as part of a conspiracy, probably cooked up by the Koch brothers' ancestors, to make out that in the Middle Ages Greenland was warmer than it is today in order to justify the vile exploitation of Mother Gaia by the evil fossil fuel industry?

GREENPEACE

Of course, the more accurate name would be Redwar. *Red* for the ideology, *war* for the *modus operandi*. This, after all, is what Greenpeace is really about: not so much saving the environment as bringing down Western industrial civilization by whatever means necessary.

It wasn't always this way. When Canadian Patrick Moore co-founded the organization in the early 1970s, Greenpeace really was about unimpeachably *nice* things like stopping pollution and saving whales. The nasty stuff came later, as the charity abandoned its core values, got hijacked by hard-left ideologues, and turned into the shrill, hectoring, anti-capitalist mega-corporation it is today.

Fighting capitalism is big business: in 2011 Greenpeace brought in global revenues of $336 million. As blogger Matthew Nisbet noted, that puts it in a similar financial league to some of the world's richest sports franchises (Arsenal Football Club; Boston Red Sox; Los Angeles Lakers). It's also more than $100 million above the American Petroleum Institute's annual revenues. So much for the mighty power of Big Oil.

How does Greenpeace make its money? By spreading fear, mainly: melting ice caps, soon-to-be extinct polar bears, rising sea levels—it's all part of Greenpeace's lucrative litany of woe.

Few of its histrionic claims, of course, bear any resemblance to observed reality. In 1995, for example, Greenpeace was forced to apologize after being caught out lying during a noisy, highly damaging

G

campaign against Shell. The oil company had wanted to dispose of an oil rig—*Brent Spar*—by sinking it deep in the Atlantic. Greenpeace used this as an excuse to launch a Europe-wide campaign to boycott Shell gas stations, claiming the rig was full of toxic residues and would cause immense environmental damage.

Yet as the UK's Natural Environmental Research Council confirmed afterwards, Shell's disposal plan was by far the most eco-friendly option. It was also—funnily enough— the option that Greenpeace had itself chosen ten years earlier when its ship, *Rainbow Warrior*, was blown up by French saboteurs: Greenpeace chose to sink it offshore so as to act as a marine habitat. One rule for hateful, capitalist oil companies, it would seem; quite another if you're a caring eco-charity.

This was just the kind of dishonesty and hypocrisy which caused Moore to quit in disgust. By the mid-1980s, he noted, none of his fellow directors had a "formal science education" but were either "political activists or environmental entrepreneurs" who had "abandoned scientific objectivity in favor of political agendas."

Greenpeace appears to have few qualms about this. In 2009, its then director Gerd Leipold was asked in an interview why in a press release it had grotesquely exaggerated the extent of ice melting off the Arctic (Greenpeace had claimed it would all be gone by 2030). "We as a pressure group have to emotionalize the issue and we're not ashamed of emotionalizing issues," said Leipold.

"Emotionalizing issues." Or, as the less enlightened among us might call it, *barefaced lying*.

G

Greenwashing

Did you know that this book was printed on 100 percent recycled, acid-free paper grown in sustainable forests using all-natural squid's ink gently harvested using a patented organic and bio-friendly technique which causes no harm whatsoever to any living creature? And were you aware that the entire production process was carbon-neutral and that all profits will be donated to rehabilitating displaced baby orangutans in the forests of Borneo?

Me neither.

G

HAECKEL, ERNST (*See also* ECOLOGY)

German naturalist who, in 1866, invented the future junk-science of Ecology ("*Oekologie*") and came up with several evolutionary theories that are now considered embarrassing—as the global warming scam eventually will be.

HANSEN, JAMES "JIM"

Former director, NASA Goddard Institute for Space Studies; adjunct professor in Department of Earth and Environmental Sciences at Columbia; climate activist; tireless proponent of "man-made global warming" theory.

"The person who is really responsible for this overestimate of global warming is Jim Hansen. He consistently exaggerates all the dangers.... Hansen has turned his science into ideology." —Dr. Freeman Dyson, physicist and mathematician

In 1988, NASA's Dr. Jim Hansen launched the global warming scare almost singlehandedly by declaring before a packed congressional hearing, as sweat visibly poured from his brow, that "the earth is warmer in 1988 than at any time in the history of instrumental measurements."

This claim was disowned by his former supervisor Dr. John Theon, who felt Hansen had "embarrassed NASA." So, too, was Hansen's claim that he had been "muzzled" by the Bush administration: a complaint

that didn't quite accord with the fact that during that period he had given 1,400 on-the-job media interviews. But Hansen's principled determination never to allow the truth to intrude on a good story has done little harm either to his career or his reputation.

Or, indeed, his bank balance—as investigative lawyer and author Chris Horner of the American Tradition Institute has noted. In the five years up to 2011, Hansen received $1.6 million in direct cash income for work related to his public service as NASA's resident global warming activist. This was over and above his NASA salary. Nor does it include the tens of thousands of dollars worth of first- and business-class travel paid to him by outside parties in order to fete him for his wisdom and expertise, at locations from London, Paris, Rome, Oslo, Tokyo, the Austrian Alps, Bilbao, California, and Australia.

Funded by Big Oil? Pah!

If it's fame, fortune, and ritzy vacations you want, you've got to get into bed with Big Eco.

Heartland Institute

Illinois-based think tank best known for its annual climate skeptics' conference.

Warmists are welcome, too—they're forever being invited, but they almost never show up, presumably because America's heartland is one area they wouldn't mind seeing fry.

HITLER, ADOLF

Vegetarian, anti-smoker, environmentalist, keenly aware of overpopulation issues, land use, and scarce resources (*Lebensraum*), supported by brown-shirt wearing lads who loved to go hiking in the woods.

HOAX (*See* CLIMATE CHANGE; GLOBAL WARMING)

HOBGOBLINS

"The whole aim of practical politics is to keep the populace alarmed (and thence clamorous to be led to safety) by menacing it with an endless series of hobgoblins, all of them imaginary." —H. L. Mencken

HOT AIR

Driving force of global warming (*see* Gore, Al).

HUTS

Wattle-and-daub structures, not terribly enviro-friendly given their reliance on fire for heat and cooking, but what we'll be reduced to if the Warmists' anti-capitalist crusade succeeds.

INCANDESCENT LIGHT BULBS

I liked incandescent light bulbs. They were warm, they were bright, they didn't flicker, they didn't give you headaches, they didn't take five hours to get going after you turned on the light switch, they didn't require you to put on a Hazchem suit if ever you accidentally broke one. And, best of all, they let you see what you were doing.

Not so the grim, low-energy eco-bulbs which we're all forced to use now, whether we like it or not.

Whatever happened to freedom of choice? Isn't that how, traditionally, we determine these issues in the capitalist West? We give the consumer a range of options—say, nice, bright, cheap light bulbs on the one hand; ugly, expensive, deadly ones full of mercury on the other—and then let the consumer decide.

Apparently, though, on this one, someone forgot to tell the regulatory authorities who've decided to go with the ban almost nobody wanted save a few fascistic greenies.

And do you know how we can tell almost nobody wanted it?

Because, for perhaps the first time ever outside wartime, the citizens of the free world are having to buy the goods they want (100W lightbulbs; 150W ones for the real diehards) on the black market and stockpile them secretly in their cupboards.

Nice work, Eco-Fascists!

INTERGOVERNMENTAL PANEL ON CLIMATE CHANGE (IPCC)

The "gold standard" of international climate science, according President Obama. Produces the *Assessment Reports* that give governments just the excuse they were looking for to raise taxes

and increase regulation, even as they snatch credit for saving the world from the greatest threat it has ever known…

All you need to know about the IPCC:

- It was set up in a fit of panic in 1988 when people were actually still gullible enough to believe stuff like "Humanity is conducting an unintended, uncontrolled, globally pervasive experiment whose ultimate consequences could be second only to nuclear war."

- It's currently run by a yoga-loving, ice-shunning, soft-porn-writing bearded railway engineer (*see* Pachauri, Rajendra).

- Its purpose is to assess evidence for "human-induced climate change," to assess human-induced climate change's likely impacts, and to recommend ways to mitigate that human-induced climate change. Can you see why it might not be in the IPCC's interests for it ever to discover that "human-induced climate change" isn't a problem?

- On each of the IPCC's five assessment reports, its certainty about the dangers of "human-induced climate change" has grown stronger. Yet, mysteriously during the same period, the real-world evidence for this has grown weaker.

- Its reports are sometimes written by green activists, teenagers, and scientists with no expertise in the relevant field (for an example of this, *see* Malaria). Imagine how terrifying it would be if, in these amateurs' hands, lay the future of the global economy, your livelihood, your liberty, and your children's chances of ever finding a job….

IT'S THE SUN, STUPID

Okay, so you're completely unqualified to talk about climate "science." I'm unqualified, too. But suppose, from your position of total benighted ignorance, you had to hazard a layman's guess as to the main driver of climate change.

Would it be:

a)   cow farts, rich capitalists flying around
      in private jets, people who don't want
      wind farms in their back yard?

      or

b)   the great burning orb in the sky?

What Churchill once said about Americans—
that they can always be counted on to do the right thing, after they've
exhausted all the other possibilities—applies equally to climate "science."

For a good three decades now, climate "scientists" have exhausted
billions of dollars worth of grant funding, striving desperately to prove
that the answer to climate change is something other than the one
which has been staring us all in the face since the first caveman looked
up at the sky on a warm day and muttered a grateful "Ugglug!"

Now, one by one, scientists are capitulating to the glaringly obvious:
It's the sun, stupid.

One of the great heroes on this front is the Danish physicist Henrik
Svensmark, who theorized that "global warming" is the result of cosmic
rays (dependent on solar activity) which act as a seed for cloud formation.

We don't need to go into the details—look it up on the internet,
preferably using a search engine other than Google. What's far more
interesting—given, remember, that the whole global warming scam is
all about politics, not science—is how hard the science establishment
tried to prevent the truth getting out.

Svensmark first advanced his theory in 1996 with a colleague from
the Danish Space Research Institute. Within a day, they had been
denounced by the then-chairman of the IPCC, Bert Bolin, who said: "I
find the move from this pair extremely naïve and irresponsible." Bolin
then used his position of authority to badmouth Svensmark and ensure
that his research was denied more funding.

There it might have ended had not Svensmark been encouraged by two scientists prepared to go against the grain—physicist Nigel Calder, formerly editor of *New Scientist*, and Jasper Kirkby, a scientist at CERN, the European Organization for Nuclear Research, home of the Large Hadron Collider. With Kirkby's support, Svensmark was able to continue his experimentation at CERN.

At least he was until the warmist establishment got to hear of it and put pressure on the CERN bureaucracy to scrap Svensmark's unhelpful experiment. Only after nearly a decade's pleading and negotiation by Kirkby was Svensmark allowed to continue his research. Sure enough, Svensmark was right: in an experiment called CLOUD, CERN's scientists successfully demonstrated that cosmic rays promote the formation of molecules which can create the clouds which do so much to affect the earth's temperature. Since these rays are in turn controlled by the sun's magnetic field, what this means is that the sun determines the earth's temperature.

Eureka!

So how come this earth-shattering news, which effectively overturned three decades worth of global warming theorizing, wasn't announced to greater fanfare?

Because, of course, it didn't suit the warmist narrative about CO_2.

"One has to make clear that cosmic radiation is only one of many parameters," declared CERN's director general, Rolf-Dieter Heuer, doing his darnedest to kill the significance of the finding as he announced it to the world's media. Sure enough, the mainstream media followed its orders—as it usually does where "climate change" is concerned.

The most important scientific discovery in the history of global warming went largely unreported, except in the blogosphere and in one or two skeptical redoubts in the print media, such as Lawrence Solomon's *National Post* column. Most of you will have read it here first—yet another reason you were right to buy this book!

JACKSON, LISA

Former head of the Environmental Protection Agency; presidential Mini Me.

With good reason was Lisa Jackson Barack Obama's personal choice to take on the role of administrator of the Environmental Protection Agency: she shares his wholehearted commitment to junk science ("The science behind climate change is settled and human activity is responsible for global warming"), higher energy prices, and the wholesale destruction of the U.S. industrial economy.

Here is what her former colleagues had to say in a report on her performance in her old job as commissioner of the New Jersey Department of Environmental Protection: "DEP employees describe Ms. Jackson as employing a highly politicized approach to decision-making that resulted in suppression of scientific information, issuance of gag orders and threats against professional staff members who dared to voice concerns."

On Ms. Jackson's eco-friendly watch, New Jersey's environment actually got dirtier. The same report noted:

"Cases in which public health was endangered due to DEP malfeasance, including one case involving a day-care center in a former thermometer factory in which DEP failed to warn parents or workers for months about mercury contamination. Rising levels of water pollution, contamination of drinking water supplies and poisoning of wildlife with no cogent state response."

And: "The state hazardous waste clean-up program under Ms. Jackson was so mismanaged that the Bush EPA had to step in and assume control of several Superfund sites."

Yes, this is the organizational genius that the president handpicked to run a government agency of 17,000 employees and to oversee a regulatory structure that can stifle the entire U.S. economy.

As administrator of the EPA, Jackson more than lived up to her early promise. Through her skilful deployment of weapons like the Clean Air Act and National Ambient Air Quality Standards, she helped cripple the U.S. coal industry, delay the Keystone Pipeline, and have a harmless trace gas—carbon dioxide—rebranded an environmental hazard.

Jackson's reign of terror was finally brought to an end in 2013 after she was discovered to have been using a separate email account—Richard Windsor—in order to elude Freedom of Information regulations. What the 12,000 (!) emails under this name reveal is the secret cozy relationship between the EPA and hard-left lobby groups such as the Environmental Defense Fund.

JAGGER, BIANCA

Former Rolling Stones consort-turned-world-savior (see Club of Rome).

JAMES I

English king (also James VI of Scotland) who beat Hitler by three and a half centuries to the title of World's First Celebrity Anti-Smoking Campaigner.

JET PACKS, THEY PROMISED US

When I was a kid growing up in the 1970s, the future was an exciting place full of hope and promise. On a TV program called *Tomorrow's World*, we were invited weekly to marvel at all the technological treats that lay in store for us—portable telephones which operated without cords; ingenious contraptions on which one could view movies any time one wished; machines that dispensed banknotes without the need to stand in a line waiting for the teller; attack ships on fire off the shoulder of Orion.... Some of these things even came true.

But one thing they didn't predict was that instead of embracing technology we would soon reject it wholesale.

Instead of thorium reactors, we would choose windmills.

Instead of genetically modified crops, we would cleave to traditional varieties more vulnerable to disease, containing fewer nutrients, requiring more water, land, and fertilizer.

Instead of incandescent bulbs capable of delivering clear, bright, warm light, we would confine ourselves to dull, flickery ones casting a sick, yellow light perfectly useless for reading or seeing by—but absolutely first rate at engendering headaches.

This may sound odd to anyone born from the 1990s onward, but there really was a time, within living memory, when progress was something to be enjoyed, not feared. In our brighter, warmer, cheaper-to-run homes with our dazzling array of time-saving contraptions, we looked back with pity on those benighted ages past when the only nocturnal illumination was the gas lamp or the tallow candle and when central heating was but a distant dream.

What, oh, what have we done to ourselves since?

I write these words with a blinding headache. Moments ago I trod in dog mess on my kitchen floor which I might well have noticed had it not been for the poor quality of the low-wattage lighting we're all now forced to use whether we like it or not, now that higher wattage bulbs are illegal. I'm shivering, too. That's because the cost of heating has been deliberately driven skyward by government policy, partly in order for us virtuously to consume less energy, partly through all the subsidies we must pay for "renewable" energy.

They promised us jet packs. Instead, thanks to the greenies, we have been bombed back to the pre-industrial age. Welcome to the twenty-first century. If this is what the future is like, you can keep it.

JOKE (*See* CLIMATEGATE INQUIRIES)

JONES, PHIL

Climate scientist; head of the University of East Anglia's Climatic Research Unit; put his previously obscure seat of learning on the international map thanks to his starring role in Climategate emails.

"I've just completed Mike's Nature trick of adding in the real temps to each series for the last twenty years (i.e., from 1981 onwards) [and] from 1961 for Keith's to hide the decline," he wrote in a 1999 email.

Since Climategate, his career has been largely devoted to trying to persuade the world that in climate science a "trick" is not a cheat and that when the data doesn't show what you want it to show it's okay to splice data to present a tidier narrative.

Journalists
(*See also* ENVIRONMENT CORRESPONDENTS)

"They're absolutely lousy [in America]. That's true also in Europe. I don't know why they've been brainwashed."
—Physicist and mathematician Dr. Freeman Dyson on the media's abject failure to report sensibly and objectively on the climate change debate

KHMER ROUGE

Cambodian Communist Party, which under dictator Pol Pot was responsible for the Killing Fields in which two million Cambodians—around a quarter of the population— were either brutally executed or died of overwork, malnutrition, or starvation; strong contender—with Hitler's Germany—for the title "greenest government ever."

> *"It was, he said, the greatest revolution the world had ever seen. It would be written in golden letters on the pages of history: how the Cambodian people had returned to the countryside to become pure, agrarian communists relieved of all ties of family, religion and culture, devoted only to Angkar (the Organisation) and the teachings of Mao and Stalin."*
> —From the *Economist* obituary of Ieng Sary, deputy prime minister of the Khmer Rouge regime

K

KIDS

"Give me a child until he is seven and I will show you the man," said the Jesuits. The greenies have marked this lesson well.

You'll notice this pernicious cultural influence as soon as your kids start school. (Which is one reason, of course, why homeschooling is so increasingly popular in the United States.) Within a few weeks you'll find that you're living with the greenie equivalent of the Hitler Youth or the Soviet Young Pioneers: one day they'll be lecturing you on recycling or the vital importance of turning off every light; next they'll be going veggie, because this week's project has been looking at some leaflets from PETA on animal exploitation.

It starts in kindergarten. In the old days, there used to be things called "nature walks" where the purpose was to become acquainted with the names of trees and flowers, to marvel at wonders like the oak apples made by gall wasps, and to enjoy the fresh air. Not anymore. Today's nature walk equivalent is politically loaded and freighted with guilt: no longer is the natural world something to be enjoyed for its own sake, but rather another excuse to generate fear and panic in impressionable little heads about pollution, resource depletion, species loss, climate change....

Almost nowhere is safe. You'll find posters advertising recycling, sustainability, and renewable energy on the walls of even the ritziest private schools. This is: a) because it plays well with socially anxious rich Moms who need to be reassured that an "elite" education doesn't mean an uncaring one; b) because there are various schemes run by the supremely well-organized, well-funded, multi-tentacled green propaganda industry which incentivize schools by giving them stars and prizes for promoting "sustainability"; and c) private school geography and science teachers are no less immune to greenie stupidity than public school ones.

What's worrying is that the green invasion of childhood has become so all-pervasive that we've come almost to take it for granted. At a very middle-class, not avowedly political, open-air rock festival in Britain, the other day, virtually the entire children's area had been given over to Greenpeace propagandists: they ran the café; they ran the adventure playground; they were there daubing the boots of any child that passed with splodges of *green* paint.

Is this because organizations like Greenpeace are jam-packed with extra-caring, child-centric, specialist youth workers who have nothing but our kids' best interests at heart? I don't think so. What we have here is a ruthless and cynical policy strategy. The shocking part is not that they're doing it—what else do you expect of hard-left activists?—but that we allow them to get away with it.

Imagine, for a moment, the outcry there'd be if the Muslim Brotherhood ran the

K

kiddies play area, handing out veils for the girls and fake beards and Osama bin Laden–style camo jackets to the boys. Or, if Exxon were in charge of the tea tent, where you got to drink orange juice out of curly, black "oil is good for you" straws and coffee out of "I <3 Big Oil" mugs.

It would never happen. Yet when extremist environmental movements target and brainwash our kids in this way, we seem to have decided that it is somehow more acceptable. Why?

KILLING BIRDS TO SAVE THE PLANET

So the Audubon Society, the American Bird Conservancy, and the Royal Society for the Protection of Birds (RSPB) state publicly on their websites that wind power is a vital part of the battle against "climate change." The RSPB has actually erected wind turbines—and profits handsomely from them—on its own land.

Can anyone work out what's wrong here?

Well, the clue lies in the organizations' names. The Audubon Society was named after the celebrated nineteenth-century naturalist best known for his seminal (and now extremely valuable) *Birds of America* illustrations. The RSPB, as its title cunningly hints, was granted a royal charter for its work protecting *birds*. The American *Bird* Conservancy would appear to be a society dedicated to preserving birds—as opposed, to, say, massacring them.

And what do wind turbines do? They kill birds (and bats) in industrial quantities. It's probably the one thing they're really good for. Not generating electricity: they're lousy at that. Not reducing CO_2: they actually increase it. But if it's bird life you want eradicated, you really can't get much better than a wind farm. According to some estimates, they kill as many as fourteen million birds annually in the United States.

The one at Altamont, California, alone, has accounted for around 2,300 golden eagles in the last twenty-five years.

That's the other great thing for hard-core orniphobes: it's not your common or garden songbirds which wind farms tend to kill, in the main, but the really special, rare, and protected ones, raptors and migratory species like the whooping crane, the sea eagle, and, yes, even America's national bird—the bald eagle. Some species—such as Australia's Tasmanian wedge-tailed eagle—are being driven to the point of extinction by wind farms.

Here's the irony. Just over fifty years ago, the author Rachel Carson launched the modern green movement with her hugely influential bestseller, *Silent Spring.* The "Silent" in the title referred to Carson's alarmist prediction that soon all the birds would be wiped out so that no longer would we evil, selfish, planet-polluting humans get to hear their joyous song. This was the book that motivated a new generation of environmentalists like Al Gore to go out and spread their gospel of man-made climate doom. In other words, Carson's book is becoming a self-fulfilling prophecy: those birds are indeed falling silent—not despite the best efforts of environmentalists but as a direct result of them!

KNUT (*See also* DICAPRIO, LEONARDO)

Celebrity polar bear cub (now deceased), cruelly named by German zookeepers to trap unwary dyslexics.

KOCH BROTHERS

Charles and David Koch, industrialist brothers who own the second largest privately owned company in the United States and donate to conservative and libertarian think tanks including the Heritage Foundation, the Cato Institute, and the Heartland Institute.

Green definition: Merchants of Doubt; ravening beasts of the far-right apocalypse, hell-bent on hounding innocent scientists to death, terrifying science teachers into teaching lies, and using a campaign of mendacious black propaganda in order to deliberately undermine environmentalists' noble attempts to save the planet.

My definition: Free market heroes; a rare and refreshing exception to the rule that the heirs of any industrial family which makes serious money will forever bend their efforts to trying to destroy the capitalist system that got them rich in the first place.

KUHN, THOMAS

U.S. physicist, historian, science philosopher (1922–1996).

Next time some climate alarmist tries to persuade you that "the science is settled," come right back at them by quoting Thomas Kuhn. Not only will this make you look informed and well read, but it is a killer point: as Kuhn explained in his 1962 classic *The Structure of Scientific Revolutions*, the science is never settled. The idea of a "consensus" is quite alien to the way science advances.

Instead, Kuhn argued, science moves on in fits and starts. For long periods, scientists in a particular field may find themselves in general agreement. But then a revolutionary new idea will emerge and—after an initial period of resistance from scientists who, either through innate conservatism or stubbornness or professional jealousy, wish to preserve the status quo—a "paradigm shift" will occur in which the old ideas are rejected and the new ones accepted.

This is exactly what is happening to those scientists in the man-made global warming industry. The science has long since moved on. But they're resisting that paradigm shift with all their might: there's just too much money in it to let the old lie die.

KUZNETS CURVE

Economic theory which posits that environmentalism is a luxury only richer nations can afford.

Why did all the twentieth century's worst environmental disasters from Bhopal to Chernobyl to the poisoning of the Aral Sea happen in the Third World or behind the Iron Curtain? Because the poorer a country is, the less likely it is to have the money spare chasing higher safety standards or factoring eco-friendly waste disposal into their industrial plans.

The logic is inescapable: if you want a cleaner world what you need is a wealthier world. To the greenies this is anathema. One of their greatest fears is what will happen when everyone in India and China and Africa can afford a car, mains electricity, the trappings of Western civilization we take for granted. Their solution is to strive to keep the Third World in poverty but it's the exact opposite of what is needed. Economic growth is good is the message of the Environmental Kuznets Curve. No wonder the greenies loathe it so much: it offends every fiber of their anti-capitalist, puritanical, misanthropic being.

INEQUALITY

INCOME PER CAPITA

K

LACEY ACT

Another step towards pan-global Eco-Fascist tyranny.

A U.S. citizen, working in the United States, would never face prosecution for breaking a foreign-made law designed to protect the interests of foreign workers in another country. Would he?

Oh yes, he would. That's the reason why in 2009 and again in 2011, the Gibson guitar company was raided by the Feds, had valuable rosewood confiscated, and was forced to suspend operations: the company had been found in breach of a 2008 environmental amendment to the Lacey Act.

No doubt the amendment was made with the noblest of intentions: to prevent deforestation in countries like Madagascar by imposing swingeing penalties on companies found importing unlicensed exotic woods. In reality, though, what Congress did in amending the Lacey Act was endorse a protectionist scam.

Gibson's rosewood had not been illegally harvested. It's just that India's protectionist laws stipulate that rosewood for export should be finished by workers in India, whereas Gibson prefers to have its own skilled workers finish it in the United States. Thanks to that Lacey Act amendment, we have a crazy situation where foreign protectionism takes precedence over the interests of American workers.

LANGUAGE

"War is peace; freedom is slavery; ignorance is strength," wrote George Orwell in *1984*.

For the greenies, that book isn't so much a dystopian satire as an operations manual. Consider the extent to which their vocabulary depends on making seriously unpleasant things sound like desirable, cozy ones, for example:

- Communistic wealth redistribution, hyper-regulation, and falling living standards: *sustainability*

- Food riots, Third World starvation, orangutan displacement, rainforest destruction: *biofuels*

- State rationing, more expensive energy delivered not when you need it but when the supplier decides: *smart grid*

- Deliberately engineered economic stagnation: *smart growth*

- Red: *green*

- Inefficient, costly power which destroys the environment, kills fish, birds, and bats, and enriches corporate fat cats at the expense of the poor: *renewable energy*

- Teenage environmental activist producing junk-science reports for the IPCC: *climate expert*

- Bird-slicing, bat-chomping death zone: *wind park*

LEE, JAMES (*See also* BIODIVERSITY; UNABOMBER)

Passionate environmentalist who in September 2010 so loved the planet that he entered the Discovery Channel's HQ with explosives strapped to his body and took three hostages before being shot dead by police.

Here are some excerpts from the manifesto James Lee posted on the internet before he died.

"The humans? The planet does not need humans. You MUST KNOW the human population is behind all the pollution and problems in the world, and YET you encourage the exact opposite instead of discouraging human growth and procreation. Surely you MUST ALREADY KNOW this!"

"Saving the environment and the remaning [sic] species diversity of the planet is now your mindset. Nothing is more important than saving them. The Lions, Tigers, Giraffes, Elephants, Froggies, Turtles, Apes, Raccoons, Beetles, Ants, Sharks, Bears, and, of course, the Squirrels."

Oh, the tragedy! The waste! With opinions like that, Lee could have become a tenured professor of conservation biology, or a bestselling environment author, or a presenter on Discovery Channel's sister channel, Animal Planet....

LFTR (LIQUID FLUORIDE THORIUM REACTOR)

Thorium is a naturally occurring nuclear fuel that is four times more common than uranium. It is so energy dense that just 5,000 tons is all that would be needed to power the earth's entire energy needs for a year.

To put this in perspective, here is how much fossil fuel was used in 2007: five billion tons of coal; thirty-one billion barrels of oil, five trillion cubic meters of natural gas; 65,000 tons of uranium. To repeat, 5,000 tons of thorium would do the job just as well.

What's more, thorium is much safer than uranium- or plutonium-powered reactors (which were largely a by-product of the nuclear arms race). A liquid fluoride thorium reactor (LFTR) does not have to operate at high pressure; it does not rely on water for coolant (hence no risk of meltdown); there are no long-term waste storage issues.

There is so much thorium in the world and it is so energy-intense that we have enough to last us, pretty much, forever. If true conservatives ever come back in power, and true science ever gets a look-in, the greenies will end up on the dustbin of history ... to be recycled, of course.

LIFESTYLE, TOO SELFISH TO CHANGE YOUR

Charge routinely leveled by greenies at all those reactionary conservatives who:

- *Insist on taking showers more than once a fortnight;*

- *Persist in eating meat;*

- *Wantonly deploy their central heating in cold weather and air-con in hot weather;*

- *Recklessly drink their water served with ice;*

- *Neglect to have themselves sterilised lest they inadvertently breed and contribute to overpopulation;*

- *Stubbornly refuse to execute their pets, despite overwhelming evidence that their methane emissions and meat consumption are partly responsible for global warming;*

- *Fail to punish themselves for their climate denialism and persistent and wanton use of scarce resources by committing suicide.*

LOGICAL FALLACIES

A logical fallacy is a dirty trick frequently used by climate alarmists and other charlatans to try to distract from the fact that their arguments are so weak. Here are some of their favorites:

Ad hominem—attacking the man not the argument—e.g., "James Delingpole is a stupid, upper class idiot who only got a second-class degree in English literature so why should we trust what he says about global warming?"

Response: yes, and Hitler was a dog-lover. Does that discredit the case for liking dogs?

Argumentum ad populum—where we are asked to believe a proposition simply because lots of people agree with it—e.g. "Everyone knows global warming is real."

Response: yes, and in times past everyone knew that if you got past the sea monsters and sailed to the end of the world, you'd fall off the edge. Did weight-of-numbers make their theory right?

Argumentum ad verecundiam (appeal to authority)—where a claim is deemed true because of the authority of the person (or institution) asserting it—e.g. "Okay, so who are you going to trust on global warming: James Delingpole or NASA, the IPCC, and the National Academy of Sciences?"

Response: throughout history, expert opinion has been wrong on any number of scientific theories from phlogiston to tectonic plates to the cause of stomach ulcers.

Motive Fallacy—questioning the motives of an argument's proposer— e.g. "Climate skeptic organizations fund events where James Delingpole speaks occasionally, so of course he's going to deny global warming."

Response: Jamie Whyte puts it best in his *Bad Thoughts: A Guide to Clear Thinking*: "A man may stand to gain a great deal of peace and quiet from telling his wife that he loves her. But he may really love her nevertheless."

LOVEJOY, THOMAS
(*See also* BIODIVERSITY; REVERSE CASSANDRA EFFECT)

Conservation biologist who popularised the term "biodiversity"; biodiversity chair of the H. John Heinz III Center for Science, Economics and the Environment; professor of Environmental Science and Policy, George Mason University; chair of the Scientific Technical Advisory Panel for the Global Environment Facility.

Biodiversity has been good to Dr. Thomas Lovejoy. It has brought him international fame, tenure, prestige, a slew of awards (including the Blue Planet Prize for being "the first scientist to academically clarify how humans are causing habitat fragmentation and pushing biological diversity towards crisis"), and a sizeable income. Better still, he has had a newly discovered parasitical wasp species that preys on butterfly larvae—*Polycyrtus lovejoyi*— named in his honor.

But what exactly has he done to merit it?

Lovejoy rose to prominence largely a result of his dramatic, attention-grabbing predictions of widespread species extinction. In 1979, he announced at a symposium that he had made "an estimate of extinctions that will take place between now and the end of the century. Attempting to be conservative wherever possible, I still came up with a reduction of global diversity between one-seventh and one-fifth."

In his contribution to *Global 2000 Report to the President* in 1980, he asserted that between 1980 and 2000, "Extinctions of plant and animal species will increase dramatically. Hundreds of thousands of species – perhaps as many as 20 percent of all species on earth—will be irretrievably lost as their habitats vanish especially in tropical forests."

A decade later, the BBC invited him to repeat these claims in his 1990 Reith Lecture. "We are in deep trouble biologically and already into a spasm of extinction of our own making unequalled since the one which took the dinosaurs. It is not a peaceable kingdom. The rate at which species disappear is about 1,000 to 10,000 times normal, and a quarter or more of all species could vanish within a couple of decades. There is a major problem with biological diversity. That really is a given."

Except (*see* Extinction Rate), it's not a "given" at all. On the contrary, real world data tells an entirely different story.

Like Paul Ehrlich, it would seem that Lovejoy is yet another beneficiary of the Reverse-Cassandra Effect: his reward for being consistently wrong with his predictions has been to be showered with glory.

On the micro scale, this might not matter overmuch. In this world, there is little correlation between honesty and reward. The real issue are the macro consequences: the dozens of Mini Me's who have studied under Lovejoy and who are now in academe or other positions of authority disseminating this junk science as gospel truth.

Low Frequency Noise

Yet another reason to hate wind turbines. They produce Low Frequency Noise which, though inaudible, causes any number of health problems in humans (and pets and livestock), ranging from balance issues and panic attacks to raised cortisol levels and depression. But maybe that's the idea: the greenies want to drive us mad as they are.

MAFIA

Biggest investor in the wind "industry" in southern Italy and Sicily; around one third of Sicily's wind farms—along with several solar plants—have been seized by the authorities investigating mafia involvement in renewable energy projects.

Green energy programs are particularly attractive to organized criminals, as Bryan Leyland of New Zealand's Climate Science Coalition explains: "Carbon trading is the only commodity trading where it is impossible to establish with reasonable accuracy how much is being bought and sold where the commodity that is traded is invisible and can perform no useful purpose for the purchaser, and where both parties benefit if the quantities traded have been exaggerated. It is, therefore, an open invitation to fraud and that is exactly what is happening all over the world."

MALARIA

According to the IPCC, malaria is one of the many plagues which will increase as a result of man-made global warming—perhaps by as many as sixty million to eighty million cases per year. This claim caused the world's leading authority on mosquito-born diseases—Dr. Paul Reiter of the Pasteur Institute—to resign in disgust from the IPCC. It completely contradicted what he told the IPCC as one of its expert contributing authors.

In fact, as Reiter had tried to explain, malaria is not heat-dependent. One of the worst outbreaks happened in frozen Siberia, and there is no evidence that malaria is increasing as a result of "climate change."

But Reiter's opinions were ignored in favor of those of his fellow authors, two of whom were full-time environmental activists; another's main contributions to science had been papers on the effectiveness of motorcycle helmets and the health effects of cell phones. Not one of the paper's lead authors had ever written a research paper on mosquito-borne diseases.

MALDIVES, THE

The Maldives are a group of low-lying coral islands in the Indian Ocean which, depending on your point of view, are either in imminent danger of being submerged by rising sea levels caused by man-made global warming or good for at least a few more centuries of ultra high-end tourism where, for the approximate price per night of the GDP of Paraguay, you get to sleep in a hut on stilts and go snorkeling before breakfast without even having to get your feet sandy.

Apparently, the Maldives government hasn't quite made up its mind either. On the one hand, in 2009, it posed for a cabinet meeting, underwater, with all the ministers behind their desks wearing scuba equipment in order to highlight the threat of climate change. On the other, it has recently invested in building eleven new airports—which isn't normally the behavior of a nation about to be drowned. Unless, perhaps, it's all for the Last Days of Saigon–style VIP evacuation of the imperiled Maldives cabinet.

MALDIVESGATE

In 2011, a deeply irresponsible, "denier" journalist caused an international diplomatic incident by claiming that the Maldives were to be excluded from the next *Times Atlas of the World* (q.v.), in recognition of their imminent disappearance due to man-made global warming.

It was meant to be a satire, but the Maldives press took it seriously, prompting a complaint from the Maldives High Commissioner in London and a demand for an apology from the newspaper which published the offending spoof.

Modesty forbids me from naming the "denier" journalist. I just hope he is properly ashamed, don't you?

MALTHUS, THOMAS

Clergyman (1766 to 1834); epically wrong doomsday merchant; eighteenth-century forerunner to Rachel Carson and Paul Ehrlich.

Malthus discovered early on that no one ever got rich by underestimating the public's appetite for scary scenarios. His 1798 *Essay on the Principle of Population* can be summed up in one sentence. "We're doomed, I tell you. Dooooomed!" (Oh, all right, two sentences.) Inevitably it ran to numerous editions, earning Malthus a lot more than his stipend as a clergyman—and possibly, too, a claim to being the founding prophet of the modern global green religion.

He observed—or claimed to observe— "the constant tendency in all animated life to increase beyond the nourishment prepared for it." What he didn't factor in—the enviro-loons never do—is that humans are not like elephants in the Serengeti, subject to massive population explosions followed by catastrophic collapse. We're a lot more inventive than that.

And so it came to pass, as Malthus had predicted, that population grew and grew. Between 1780 and 1914, Britain's population swelled fourfold. But the other stuff he predicted—the starvation, disease, war, and vice which he thought inevitably accompany overpopulation—did not. In that same period, Britain's economy grew thirteen-fold, more than accommodating the needs of all these extra people Malthus had warned us about. Indeed, pretty much everyone ended up better clothed, better housed, better educated than at any time in history. Malthus, understandably, fell out of fashion.

But then, a hundred or so years after his death, two kids were playing in a graveyard. Their names were Rachel [Carson] and Paul [Ehrlich]. "Hey," said Rachel. "Looks like we've just found ourselves a totally discredited philosophy." "Cool!" said Paul. "Let's dig it up...."

MANBEARPIG

Terrifying beast—"half man, half bear, and half pig"—which roams the earth attacking humans for no reason whatsoever. At least, according to Al Gore when he comes to lecture at South Park Elementary School to warn the students about the latest deadly environmental threat. Unfortunately, no one will take Gore seriously—even though, as he frequently declares  "I'm cereal. I'm super-cereal." Apart from dismissing his views on global warming, *South Park* was here mocking a recent appearance by Gore on the *Oprah Winfrey Show*, where he had misunderstood a question regarding his favorite cereal. The phrase has haunted him ever since.

MANN, MICHAEL (*See also* HOCKEY STICK)

Formerly: The most famous climate scientist in the world thanks to his widely publicized, oft-reproduced, Al Gore–endorsed, schoolchildren-scaring, politician-galvanizing Hockey Stick.

Today: Comedy character; litigant; Freedom of Information fugitive; standing joke, best known for his starring role in the YouTube hit song by Minnesotans for Global Warming, "Hide the Decline."

M

MARX, KARL

Invented Marxism.

Karl Marx.

Karl Marx may well be responsible for many bad things—earnest sociology lecturers; Occupy Wall Street; the Soviet Union; Barack Obama—but environmentalist nonsense isn't one of them. Indeed, were Marx alive today, he would likely be fighting shoulder to shoulder with the capitalists against the eco-loons. We know this because in his lifetime Marx was a severe critic of Malthus—whose essay he called a "libel against the human race." The collapse of capitalism might be inevitable, he believed, but it certainly wouldn't be the result of population growth outstripping scarce resources.

Marx's co-author, Friedrich Engels, was similarly skeptical. In his 1844 essay "The Myth of Overpopulation," he noted that while the total area of land might be finite, and while additional labor might not always yield a proportionate increase in output, there was a third element which "the economists, however, never consider as important": science.

"What is impossible for science?" Engels asked.

The warming lobby would agree up to a point. Nothing is impossible for "science" because when its data doesn't suit your purposes, you can always make it up.

MAUNDER MINIMUM

Solar minimum (1645 to 1715).

Yes, it really was colder during the Little Ice Age. This was when the ice froze thick enough on the River Thames to hold fairs on top of it. Greenies will tell you that this is because the river flowed more slowly back then and was therefore more susceptible to freezing. Nope: it was because the era coincided with low sun spot activity. Just like the new solar minimum we're entering now. Brrr!

MCINTYRE, STEVE, AND MCKITRICK, ROSS— OR, HOW TWO OUTSIDERS TOOK ON THE CLIMATE ESTABLISHMENT AND WON

No man has worked harder to expose the global warming scam than the unassuming, tatty-sweater-wearing, squash-obsessed, ex-mining engineer Steve McIntyre. Climate skeptics are often accused of being ideologically motivated. But McIntyre is neither a man of the Right (he's a socialist), nor a "denier" of man-made global warming. He just happens to have an unusually scrupulous regard for facts, hard data, and solid evidence—born of his career in a field where there is no room for error: in both mining and engineering, sloppiness costs lives.

Despite the much fine work he has done since on his website Climate Audit, McIntyre remains best known as destroyer of what for a period was the central plank in the alarmists' case for Catastrophic Anthropogenic Global Warming: Michael Mann's Hockey Stick graph.

It began out of a prize-winning mathematician's pure intellectual curiosity. How, McIntyre idly wondered, did the experts know that 1998 was—or so they claimed—the warmest year of the millennium?

His investigation led him into the murky science of paleoclimatology—in which "proxy data," such as the rings on very old trees, are used to try to estimate past climate temperatures. It's an imprecise art with plenty of margin for error and cherry-picking manipulation. And this, it struck McIntyre, was a problem.

McIntyre's suspicions hardened when he tried to replicate the most famous of all climatological reconstructions, only to find himself being continually obstructed and stonewalled by its creator Michael Mann. If it couldn't be reproduced by an independent observer, how could it be scientifically valid, McIntyre wanted to know. Mann's response was to accuse McIntyre of harassment. He was supported by many of his friends in the science and political establishment—who all appeared to

M

agree that such important research was best left to the "experts" rather than meddling amateurs with no specialist track record.

Undeterred, McIntyre pressed ahead with his investigations, now assisted by fellow Canadian Ross McKitrick, an environmental economist at the University of Guelph. Over the next months and years, they discovered several shocking things which would not only make a mockery of Mann's much-hyped graph, but also of by far the strongest "evidence" in the case for man-made global warming.

Mann's graph, they discovered, relied on a computer algorithm so skewed that it would produce a hockey stick shape more than 99 percent of the time, regardless of what data you fed into it. Furthermore, the scary uptick at the end of the chart—making it look like an ice hockey stick—had been derived by overemphasising data from one type of tree, the bristlecone pine, which is widely acknowledged to be an unreliable indicator of twentieth-century climate change.

In other words, Mann had fudged it. And been comprehensively debunked by two amateur sleuths.

MEDIEVAL WARM PERIOD (MWP)

Bounteous period of global warmth and fruitfulness, when Greenland was green and grapes flourished north of Hadrian's Wall (900 AD to 1280 AD).

Stalin wanted to airbrush class traitors out of his history. Alarmists want to do the same with the MWP. Here's their problem: not one single person, not even the ritziest king, emperor, or pope was cruising round the Middle Ages in a 4x4 with tinted windows, nor did they fly private jets, nor was there any heavy industry belching out CO_2. Yet, amazingly, the overwhelming evidence suggests that despite all this, the climate was warmer in medieval times than it is now.

Wow! Could this mean, perchance, that maybe there are more significant drivers of global climate than human carbon emissions?

You might think so, I might think so, but the Warmists would much rather you didn't.

"We have to get rid of the MWP," a leading climate was once overheard saying. IPCC lead author Jonathan Overpeck denies ever having said this. Apparently he just wanted to "nail" it—or "deal it a mortal blow." Which, of course, isn't the same thing at all. Is it?

MERCHANTS OF DOUBT

Pseudo-academic thesis by greenie pseudo-academic (is there any other kind?) Naomi Oreskes, professor of History and Science Studies at the University of California, San Diego.

Apparently, the reason skepticism about global warming is growing is because a handful of high-placed shill scientists in the pay of the fossil fuel industry, Big Tobacco, and sundry think tanks from the Vast Right-Wing Conspiracy, have used their power and influence to sow doubt in the public's imagination about the existence of man-made climate change. So argue Oreskes (and her co-author Erik Conway) in their book, *Merchants of Doubt*.

But those right-wing conspirators were even more evil than Oreskes and Conway give them credit for. As well as corrupting public opinion, they actually managed to get global warming *to stop for sixteen years*, thus giving the dangerous impression that there was a scientific basis for their lies! Is there no end to the cleverness of the Vast Right-Wing Conspiracy?

METHANE HYDRATE (*See also* SHALE GAS)

Miracle fossil fuel known as "burning ice." These cold, crystal-like structures of ethane and water represent by far the biggest reserve of hydrocarbons within the earth's crust. When greenies get to hear of their existence, they're going to hate methane hydrate even more than shale gas.

Why are they going to hate it so? Well, one, it's a fossil fuel—and fossil fuels are, as we know, really, really evil, m'kay. And two, there's lots of it—so much that in the United States there's enough of the stuff to supply America's gas needs for the next 1,000 years.

Now, imagine how upsetting this will be if you're blindly wedded to the idea that fossil fuels are going to run out imminently and that we must guard them jealously for future generations.

Only a thousand years of supplies left? However are those helpless people in 2114 going to survive?

Better build wind farms now!

MISANTHROPY

"The common enemy of humanity is man. In searching for a new enemy to unite us, we came up with the idea that pollution, the threat of global warming, water shortages, famine and the like would fit the bill. All these dangers are caused by human intervention, and it is only through changed attitudes and behaviour that they can be overcome. The real enemy, then, is humanity itself."
—*The First Global Revolution* published by the Club of Rome (q.v.), 1993

MISMANAGEMENT

Have you noticed how state-managed housing projects are so much prettier, cleaner, safer, and better tended than homes belonging to private property owners? And how, if you want a business to be run really efficiently, local government always makes a much better job of it than private enterprise?

Me neither. It's why we should all be deeply suspicious whenever private land is purchased (or confiscated) by the state in order to preserve it for the benefit of future generations. As Holly Fretwell confirms in her book *Who Is Minding the Federal Estate? Political Management of America's Public Lands*, the result is inevitably disastrous.

The problem is threefold—ideology, money, incompetence.

First ideology: once in government hands, the land falls victim to the warped, anti-scientific values of all those environmental "experts" who still subscribe to discredited theories like "steady-state" ecology. They believe that land left to its own devices—so, no grazing by livestock; no forestry—does best. In fact, though, the opposite is true.

Second, money. From 1965 to 2002, the Land and Water Conservation Fund (LWCF) provided nearly $12.5 billion for land acquisition by the government. But the costs of maintaining that land are $224 billion, which the government simply cannot afford.

Third, incompetence. The Bureau of Land Management, which manages 264 million acres of the American heartland, full of potential resources and tourism revenue that should turn a profit, instead loses so much money that it claims not to have enough for maintenance.

The combination is toxic, as we can see from the fate of all those acres of forest that have been set aside—mothballed—to save rare species like the Spotted Owl. According to the Forest Service, between ninety and 200 million acres of western forest are in danger of being consumed by a once-in-a-millennium fire so hot it will cause irreparable damage not just to the trees but the subsoil and the seeds buried underneath. Why? Because strict environmental regulation allows no thinning or cleaning up deadfall, let alone clear-cutting or logging.

This lack of maintenance has led to spindly, unhealthy trees riddled with root rot, pine beetle, and budworm. Overgrown forests have reduced by as much as 50 percent the water flow to communities and farms below. Dense, uncleared forests—with deadfall (shed branches and other detritus) up to twenty feet high—and a concomitant dearth of meadows have made these forests no-go zones for elk and antelope and their predators.

Environmentalists are not conserving the American landscape with their well-intended preservation methods. They are killing it. And all

M

because they cannot seem to realize that man is a natural part of the environment, too—and not just man as some imagined primitive, but man as forester and farmer, rancher and recreator, miner and minder of the natural world. As the late marine biologist, atomic energy commissioner, and governor of Washington state (and conservative Democrat) Dixy Lee Ray famously said, "A well-tended garden is better than a neglected woodlot."

NASA

Formerly: embodiment of the American can-do spirit; the institution that won the race to put the first man on the moon.

Now: embodiment of the American can't-do spirit; the institution which has put its Mars mission on hold in order to spend more time promoting Islamic outreach and global warming.

In 1969, the United States squandered $25 billion on the first manned lunar landing. Never mind the ugly, permanent footprints with which the vandal Neil Armstrong ravaged that virgin moon dust: What about the *carbon* footprint, did no one think of that? How many polar bears had their habitats jeopardized by the nearly 2,200 tons of rocket fuel used to send that typically phallocentric projectile into space? What about all the ecology programs, all the solar energy start-ups, all the Snail Darter and Little Owl research initiatives which could have been funded by that wasted money?

And what about the inequality created by the invention of Teflon—leading to a cruelly divided world in which rich Westerners could for ever more fry their eggs on non-stick pans while those in the developing world had to endure the ongoing misery and pain of watching their fried eggs (if they could even afford eggs) stick to stainless steel, aluminium, or cast-iron pans, with the constant threat of broken-yolk misery?

Happily, we know better now.

Today, thanks to its Goddard Institute for Space Studies (GISS), NASA has become one of the world's foremost proponents of climate change alarmism. GISS provides one of the four main global temperature records—and, thanks to the expert adjustments of its former director Dr. James Hansen—shows more extreme warming than any other. Indeed, some misguided critics, failing to understand that Hansen is serving a "truth" far higher than mere objective reality, have accused him of outright dishonesty.

In 2007, for example, GISS was forced to revise its figures after Hansen was caught out adjusting U.S. surface temperature data to make earlier years look cooler and later years warmer in order to make "global warming" seem more dramatic and extreme. Hansen had claimed that the 1990s were the hottest decade in twentieth-century America, when in fact the unadjusted data showed that the 1930s were the hottest.

Undeterred by this embarrassment, GISS found an ingenious new way to show the world was getting warmer. In 2010—in defiance of rival data sets which showed global temperatures dropping sharply—GISS's record showed that temperatures had shot up by 0.2 Celsius. On closer examination, however, it emerged that only 25 percent of the figures were based on actual temperature readings. The rest were completely made up.

NATURALISM (*See also* ECOLOGY)

The kind of guilt-free study of nature that they just don't do anymore....

NAZIS: HOW GREEN WERE THEY?

Very. They beat even David Cameron to the title of "greenest government ever." They were the first to ban smoking on public transport (Hitler thought it a filthy habit: tobacco, he believed, was "the wrath of the Red Man against the White Man, vengeance for having been given hard liquor"). They were the first to take "animal rights" seriously (in 1933, Goering said that anyone found guilty of animal cruelty or experimentation should be sent to concentration camps). They passed the first national environmental laws: the Reich Nature Protection Law of 1935. They were the first to champion organic food (Heinrich Himmler wanted to feed his SS on nothing else—till it emerged that this wasn't technically feasible, organic food requiring so much more land than that using artificial fertilizer).

And, of course, they were the first modern Western nation to deal—with mechanized, characteristic German efficiency—with that issue of such passionate concern to so many in the environmental movement then and now. The—ahem—*overpopulation* problem.

But shh! Don't mention this to the greenies. They might invoke Godwin's Law (q.v.).

NEW WORLD ORDER

Ultimate goal of the green movement; but obviously you can never say this or you'd sound like a Conspiracy Theorist (q.v.). On the other hand....

The Earth Charter (2000), co-written by Maurice Strong and former Soviet president Mikhail Gorbachev, calls for the replacement of sovereign states by an "Earth Government," which ensures "that all trade supports sustainable resource use, environmental protection and progressive labour standards."

And: "I believe that the new world order will not be fully realised unless the United Nations and its Security Council create structures ... authorised to impose sanctions and make use of other measures of compulsion." —Speech by Gorbachev on ecology, 1992, John Findley Greed Foundation Lecture, Fulton, Missouri

And: "Please stand up, delegates of the world, hold each other's hand and let us swear together that we will accomplish this historical miracle before it is too late: to save this Earth, to save humanity with a new world order." —Former UN Assistant Secretary-General Dr. Robert Muller, who drafted much of the United Nations environmental policy

NO PRESSURE

Counterproductive snuff-video made by green pressure group 10:10.

Scene: a typical English schoolroom where a lovably, kooky teacher (played by Gillian Anderson out of *X-Files*) is asking her class how they plan to reduce their carbon emissions for an eco-campaign called 10:10.

Obviously it's not compulsory, she says, sweetly. If the children don't want to play ball, it's up to them. "No pressure."

Sundry do-good creeps in the class tell teacher what they're planning. One is going to cycle to school instead of taking the car. "That's fantastic, Jemima!" says teacher. She asks for a show of hands to see who else is going to participate. Only two children abstain: a glum-looking pair called Philip and Tracy. "That's absolutely fine," the teacher assures them. "Your own choice."

Then she reaches for a red button hidden beneath paperwork on her desk. She presses it once. Tracy explodes in a spume of pink gore. Teacher presses it again. This time it's Philip's turn to die horribly. The rest of the class screams in terror, their uniforms smeared in blood, their school room covered in the body parts of Philip and Tracy. A dismembered limb thuds onto a desk. Teacher continues, oblivious: "Now everybody please remember to read chapters five and six on glaciation. Except, for Philip and Tracy."

You can maybe see from that description why the video backfired. The amazing thing was that the people who made it, couldn't. Not director Richard Curtis (best known for such cozily safe movies as *Four Weddings and a Funeral* and *Notting Hill*); not Radiohead (who did the soundtrack); not Gillian Anderson; not the famous footballers who appeared later in the video; not the organizers of the charity whose aims—incidentally—had been publicly endorsed by everyone from prime minister David Cameron to fashion designer Nicole Farhi....

Initially released amid much fanfare, the film had to be hastily withdrawn amid a wave of public outrage. It became a viral hit on the internet, where skeptics gleefully rechristened it Splattergate.

For the environmental movement, it was indeed what the kids might call an "epic fail." Those kids, at least, who hadn't already been executed for showing insufficient concern about the deadly menace called Climate Change.

N

NOBEL PRIZE

Ironic, comedy prize awarded annually to implausible candidates by the Norwegians and Swedes to show that they have a sense of humor. Winners include: Paul Krugman (Economics!); Yasser Arafat and Barack Obama (Peace!); but the acknowledged best joke so far in the prize's history is the awarding of a prize—peace again—to masseuse-threatening Al Gore and the laugh-a-minute, "let's cut and paste some data" Intergovernmental Panel on Climate Change.

NOBLE CAUSE CORRUPTION

Affliction to which climate scientists are especially prone: If you think you're saving the world, what data won't you skew, what exaggerations won't you make, what lies won't you tell in order to prod policymakers into taking concerted action NOW?

> ## Normal Weather
>
> *"The idea of normal weather is an unfortunate legacy resulting from an idea that grew up in the early days of this century that the climate was constant. Nature doesn't know what 'normal' means."*
> —Hubert Lamb, founder of the Climatic Research Unit, University of East Anglia

NORTH KOREA

World's greenest economy: in North Korea, every day is Earth Day, with hardly anyone using electricity at any time, day or night, thus ensuring that carbon emissions per capita are kept to the barest minimum. All right, so maybe it's because the energy infrastructure is so poor, they can't afford the fuel and even if they could there's no viable industry to power it with. But let's not be too critical—they're doing their best and Kim Jong-un is definitely the kind of green hero who deserves to be mentioned in the same breath as Al Gore, George Soros, and the king of Canadian enviro-nuttery, Maurice Strong.

OBAMA, BARACK

Visionary; bi-partisan healer; unifier; freedom lover; rescuer of the U.S. economy; savior of the American Dream.

Just a few of the phrases that no future historian will ever use to describe the forty-fourth president of the United States. There is much we could say about Barack Hussein Obama. But let us confine ourselves to the passage in his Second Inaugural Address concerning "climate change." It tells you all you need to know about the man, his principles, his policies, and, worst of all, your future.

We, the people, still believe that our obligations as Americans are not just to ourselves, but to all posterity. We will respond to the threat of climate change, knowing that the failure to do so would betray our children and future generations. Some may still deny the overwhelming judgment of science, but none can avoid the devastating impact of raging fires, and crippling drought, and more powerful storms. The path towards sustainable energy sources will be long and sometimes difficult. But America cannot resist this transition; we must lead it. We cannot cede to other nations the technology that will power new jobs and new industries—we must claim its promise. That is how we will maintain our economic vitality and our national treasure—our forests and waterways; our croplands and snowcapped peaks. That is how we will preserve our planet, commanded to our care by God. That's what will lend meaning to the creed our fathers once declared.

Okay. Let's parse that.

1. "All posterity," "our children," "future generations." *If you do not agree with my plan to bomb the U.S. economy back to the Stone Age*

to remedy the non-existent problem of climate change, you are a moral vacuum, a selfish SOB, and quite possibly a child murderer, too. Expect a visit from my Department of Justice soon.

2. "Some may still deny...." *Did you see what I just did there with that "d" word? I put climate skepticism into the same category as "denying the overwhelming historical evidence that Hitler murdered six million Jews."*

3. "...the overwhelming judgment of science." *What overwhelming judgment? This a) would be news to Galileo, Newton, Einstein, and every great scientist who ever lived—all of whom confounded "the consensus," and b) is pure conjecture, anyway. How do we know the majority of scientists believe this nonsense? See Consensus? What Consensus? And in any case as Einstein among many have argued, science is not a numbers game.*

4. "... raging fires, and crippling drought, and more powerful storms." *Ah: the "Extreme Weather" meme, supported by no real world data whatsoever.*

5. "The path towards sustainable energy sources will be long and sometimes difficult...." *Of course it will because "sustainable" is environmentalese for "expensive, inefficient, taxpayer-subsidized, and unnecessary."*

6. "Transition." *Now it gets scary. "Transition" is the eco-Nazi codeword for "the deliberate, self-inflicted destruction of Western industrial civilization."*

7. "We must lead it." *Small sop of consolation there, guys. At least the New World Order is going to be run by God-fearing, apple pie–fed, all-American Eco-Fascists rather than foreign ones.*

8. "We cannot cede to other nations the technology that will power new jobs and new industries...." *Except we already have, mostly to the Chinese who consistently undercut us in "green technologies" like solar panels and wind power. Hence the death of Solyndra. Hence*

also the fact that "green jobs" don't do much to reduce American unemployment because most of them end up abroad.

9. "Our economic vitality." *Yeah, right.* See "Feeding the Masses on Unicorn Ribs."

10. "Our forests"—*Or our former forests. Now—thanks to the well-meaning intervention of environmentalists opposed to any form of management or commercial exploitation—spindly, overcrowded, tinder boxes waiting to explode.*

11. "Our croplands"—*Those few that haven't been converted to biofuels.*

12. "Snowcapped peaks"—*Which, even now, a wind farm developer somewhere near you has earmarked as the perfect spot for fifty-five hundred-feet-tall wind turbines.*

13. "That is how we will preserve our planet, commanded to our care by God."—*Do you know how dumb I think you are, Republican America? I think you're so dumb that all I have to do is invoke this God guy you're so keen on, and I'll have you eating out of the palm of my hands.*

14. "The creed our fathers once declared."—*Oh, yeah. And the Founding Fathers. Apparently you conservatives are keen on them, too. Whoever they were. Yadda yadda. Constitution. Whatever....*

OCEAN ACIDIFICATION

Ocean acidification is the Warmists' Siegfried Line—the position of retreat they've prepared for when AGW theory collapses completely and they need some other excuse to justify their attempts to finger carbon dioxide as the deadliest substance known to man.

It's not going to hold off the enemy for very long though. Ocean acidification theory has been extensively rebutted, including in studies which suggest that, far from being harmed by warmth and CO_2, coral and plankton have actually benefited from it.

My advice to starry-eyed kids doing marine biology courses at college, banking on a sociopolitically vital career of whale-watching, scuba diving, and sunbathing on the decks of research vessels on lavishly grant-funded expeditions to discover the effects of CO_2 on the reefs of Bora Bora and the Maldives: keep practicing the phrase "Would you like regular or large fries with that?"

ODUM, HOWARD AND EUGENE

U.S. ecologists: Eugene (1913–2002); Howard (1924–2002); brothers; co-authors _Fundamentals of Ecology_ (1953).

A decade before the dangerous, hugely influential junk-science of Rachel Carson's _Silent Spring_ came the dangerous, hugely influential junk-science of the Odum brothers in their standard text _Fundamentals of Ecology_. They're the ones who popularized the idea—now a key article of faith in the green movement—that the earth is divided into a series of ecosystems, each dependent on one another.

It's a neat notion, which more or less makes sense as a grand universal theory of everything. But a theory is all it remains—and a decreasingly plausible one at that.

Part of the brothers' problem was their attitude to the scientific method. Though Howard did plenty of work in the field—from the ponds of North Carolina to the tropical rainforest of Guatemala to the Pacific coral reefs—he wasn't much interested in empiricism, observation, and deduction. Instead, he'd already made up his mind how the natural world behaved: like an electrical system.

To this end, Howard drew up diagrams of the real world ecosystems he had visited, recasting them as electric circuits with feedback loops showing how energy flowed between animals and plants. From this sprung the fashionable idea that ecosystems exist naturally in a "steady state"—that is, that there is a "balance of nature," which we disturb at our peril.

The theory might look good on paper but, as one of Howard's former assistants noted, has little to do with nature. Instead, it created "a machine-like fantasy of stability." The assistant added: "Driven by the desire for prestige biological reality disappeared. Organisms were expected to react mechanically in predictable ways. Animals became robots and the ideas were never presented as hypotheses to be tested."

Do these criticisms sound vaguely familiar? They should for they might just as well be describing any of a number of the green movement's shibboleths, from Anthropogenic Global Warming to Peak Oil: it seems that for decades, now, we have been at the mercy of junk scientific theories which, not through evidence but merely through repetition, have taken on the status of unassailable truth.

OK COMPUTER

Remember how long ago it was when Radiohead released *OK Computer*? Well, that's how long it has been since there was any global warming.

It doesn't mean that "global warming" won't start again at some time in the near or distant future. But what it does mean is that any child aged sixteen or under being treated to the usual Warmist litany at school is being warned about a "problem" no less remote from their personal experience than, say, the Soviet nuclear threat, the Spanish flu epidemic, Adolf Hitler, bubonic plague, attack by Pterodactyl.

Now obviously, like any loving parent, I believe it's important that our children should be prepared to deal with every eventuality. (What if, thanks to cloning technology, that devilish Russian president Putin plans to create lots of mini-Hitlers using the body the Soviets retrieved from the Berlin Bunker in 1945? What then, eh?) On the other hand, I think we can most of us agree that there's only so much time in the school day. If our children are going to be warned about problems, shouldn't it be about ones that they are actually likely to encounter?

O

Problems, like, maybe: the distinct possibility that they're going to grow up in a world of galloping inflation, overregulation, and high unemployment, as a result of all the measures greenies have introduced to deal with a problem which has been non-existent since before they emerged from the womb?

ONO, YOKO

Avant-garde artiste; creative mastermind/inspiration behind all the best work of the Beatles who would have remained in total obscurity without her genius; environmental activist.

In recent years, Yoko Ono has turned her razor intellect, legendary personal charm, and exquisite vocal talents to raising publicity for her Artists Against Fracking. Fellow members include Mark Ruffalo, Robert De Niro, Susan Sarandon, and Rufus Wainwright, all of whom eagerly signed up to join—it is rumored—after an ultimatum by Yoko that if they didn't, she would start to sing.

OUT OF SEASON (*See also* FOOD MILES)

Eating food out of season is bad, apparently. We should learn to live as our ancestors did, before refrigeration and cheap transport ruined everything: worm-eaten apples in autumn, little but cabbage and root crops in winter, but then a growing abundance of fun things like asparagus, strawberries, and peaches as we approach the bounties of summer.

Fine, all you wholesome greenies, if that's the lifestyle you want, don't let me hold you back.

Me, I quite like all-year-round mangos and grapes and kumquats and avocadoes and whatever else takes my fancy. The technical term for this is Civilization.

OVERPOPULATION (*See also* MALTHUS, THOMAS)

Article of faith among neo-Malthusian greenies—sometimes known as the "Elephant in the Room"—that the world is getting far too crowded and that Something Must Be Done!

Greenies are very sure of the problem. There are too many of us: perhaps even as many as 6.5 billion too many if you believe Ted Turner or the Georgia Guidestones (q.v.).

What they tend to be less upfront about is how they mean to go about achieving the noble aim of clearing more space for the stick insects and the fungi and the ringworm and all the other glorious plants and creatures with whom most of us are so unworthy to share breathing space.

Still, we do have some useful historical precedents from great environmental gurus of the past. Adolf Hitler (q.v.) chose the most direct route; Rachel Carson (q.v.) did it through the more subtle means of effecting a ban on DDT (q.v.); advocates of biofuels are achieving much the same effect by helping to generate starvation in the developing world.

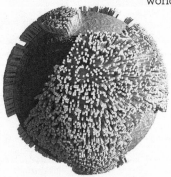

There is, of course, another solution which, for some reason, you never hear greenies discussing: encourage the developing world to get as rich as possible as quickly as possible. Wealth is the most effective form of birth control there is.

OZONE LAYER

Another global environmental disaster averted by concerted international political action brought about by green activism....

The scare began in the 1970s when scientists noticed a decline in the concentration of ozone over Antarctica and fingered chlorofluorocarbons (CFCs)—used in aerosol cans and refrigerators—as the culprit. This resulted in an international agreement to ban CFCs by 1996. But it made no difference to the ozone hole. As Matt Ridley notes: "The hole stopped growing before the ban took effect, then failed to shrink afterwards." Nobody knows why.

PACHAURI, RAJENDRA (*See also* INTERGOVERNMENTAL PANEL ON CLIMATE CHANGE)

Bearded, vegetarian, cricket-loving, soft pornography author, and railway engineer, with numerous interests in the lucrative "sustainability" industry mysteriously appointed head of the Intergovernmental Panel on Climate Change.

To appreciate just how crazy an appointment this is, try to imagine if the U.S. presidency were thrown into the hands of a "community organizer," with a hard-left voting record in elective office, who had associated with domestic terrorists and rabble-rousing pastors, who denied American exceptionalism, and intended to impose swinging new environmental taxes and regulations to stifle business and provide massive taxpayer subsidies to his friends. *That* crazy.

PAL REVIEW

When "climate scientists" invoke "peer-review" to defend their junk science, what they really mean is "pal-review": unquestioning approval for their mates; rejection for their rivals.

Here's Dr. Phil Jones in the Climategate emails caught explaining how it works:

"I can't see either of these papers being in the next IPCC report. Kevin and I will keep them out somehow—even if we have to redefine what the peer-review literature is!"

Weirdly enough, this same Phil Jones can be read elsewhere in the Climategate emails, primly declaring: "The peer-review system is the safeguard science has adopted to stop bad science being published."

"Bad science" being whatever Phil and his likeminded chums decided it is, presumably.

PASCAL'S WAGER

Pascal's Wager is often invoked by alarmists to demonstrate that we *must act now* to deal with "Climate Change," regardless of the cost. It demonstrates nothing of the kind.

The wager, devised in 1670 by the French philosopher Blaise Pascal, goes like this: even if there is no proof for the existence of God, it still makes rational sense to believe in Him because the potential losses of not believing in Him if He *does* exist are far greater than the potential costs of believing in Him if He *doesn't* exist. Worst case for the former is eternal damnation in burning hellfire. Worst case for the latter is having wasted a lifetime going to church.

You can see where the greenies are going with this one. There is, indeed, a particularly smug *USA Today* cartoon arguing much the same thing. It shows a lecturer at a climate summit. Behind him, on a board, is a list of goals he is trying to achieve: Energy Independence; Preserve Rainforests; Sustainability; Green Jobs; Livable Cities; Renewables; Clean Water, Air; Healthy Children; etc., etc. A cross-looking, middle-aged delegate—presumably one of those terrible "deniers" one reads about—says angrily: "What if it's a big hoax and we create a better world for nothing?"

The assumption behind the smug joke—as, of course, behind the invocation of Pascal's Wager—is that responding to "climate change" is cost free.

Yeah, I guess it is. So long as you don't count the higher taxes, the increased regulations, the expensive non-jobs, the lives lost to biofuels and fuel poverty, the environmental damage caused by wind and solar, the $45 trillion the International Energy Agency reckons it will cost to decarbonize the world economy by 2050....

PASSIVE SMOKING

Urban myth, promulgated by safety Nazis at institutions like the World Health Organization to justify yet another of their arbitrary, anti-democratic, puritanical assaults on property rights and human freedom.

If you're Hitler and you want to ban smoking on public transportation, you just go ahead and do it. In a democracy, however, you have to be more circumspect. That's why, when the WHO and all its friends in the health and safety industry wanted to go much further than Hitler ever did and ban smoking in all public places, they first needed a compelling reason to justify it.

The obvious one was "passive smoking." If they could prove that environmental tobacco smoke harmed non-smokers and smokers alike, then they had as good as won: no longer would it be a civil liberties issue but a public safety issue.

But there was a problem. According to the most rigorous and extensive long term investigation into the subject—by James Enstrom and Geoffrey Kabat—"passive smoking," no matter how intense and prolonged, causes no significantly increased risk of cancer or heart disease.

Fortunately, as ever, the health campaigners had a time-honored solution. It was much the same one Stalin had used to crush proponents of the discredited bourgeois science of Gregor Mendel; and the one Hitler used against the discredited Jewish science of Einstein; and it's the same one, of course, which we see being used today by the climate science establishment to suppress inconvenient research expressing scepticism about the theory of Anthropogenic Global Warming.

First, Enstrom and Kabat were cut off from their funding; next, they were accused of being in the pay of sinister interests (true, up to a point: But how else could Enstrom and Kabat continue their research except with help from the tobacco industry?); next, groups of more amenable scientists were co-opted into producing research which showed that, yes, passive smoking *is* a serious danger.

You may say that the world is a better place now that it no longer resembles a smoke-filled office from *Mad Men*. Up to a point—though I'd maintain we're definitely poorer for the departure of the three-Martini lunch—you may be right. But surely the point of living in a free society is that we get where we want to go by choice, rather through officially endorsed lies and coercion?

PEAK EVERYTHING

As Sheikh Yamani once quipped, "The Stone Age didn't end because they ran out of rocks." But I'll bet it didn't stop the cavemen worrying that it would.

Fear of running out of stuff is a perfectly natural and healthy human instinct. It happened to me once, with cold beer deprivation on a summer's day when I was at university. The experience so traumatized me that I vowed then and there never to live another day of my life without access to a fridge with cold beer in it: one of the few resolutions I have never broken. But of course, in times past, running out of stuff was a much more serious concern which could result in death by starvation, dehydration, or hypothermia.

So it's no surprise to find even the finest minds of each generation preoccupied with the problem of what economists call "scarce resources." We see it in the concerns of the Third Century theologian Tertullian that "natural elements" were running out; we see it in Malthus's (q.v.) concerns in the late eighteenth century about food shortages, in Lord Kelvin's concerns in 1902 about Peak Coal, and President Warren Harding's concerns in the 1920s about Peak Oil (q.v.)

and Peak Gas. None of these men was notably stupid; yet in each case, they could not have been more wrong. Is there not perhaps a useful historical lesson we can draw from this?

Yes, of course there is. The first lesson is: just because someone is an "expert" doesn't mean he can't be wrong. And the second lesson is—as Bjorn Lomborg was surprised to discover when he researched his *Skeptical Environmentalist*—things are rarely quite as bad as the doommongers say they are. It follows therefore that rather than base our policies on that gut feeling so many of us have that "We're running out of stuff! Help!" we should instead base them on hard evidence.

What history shows us is that long before any commodity reaches depletion point human ingenuity—driven by market forces—finds a substitute. The Age of Coal was followed by the Age of Oil; the Age of Oil will most likely be followed by the Ages of Nuclear and Shale; and so on.

While Peak Everything theory may make intuitive sense—everything runs out in the end, after all—it is an illusory problem which really need not detain us in the way so many greenies seem to think it should.

PEAK OIL

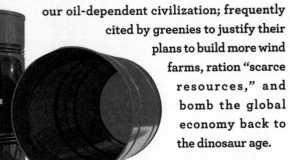

Doomsday theory that the oil is running out even faster than we think with devastating potential consequences for our oil-dependent civilization; frequently cited by greenies to justify their plans to build more wind farms, ration "scarce resources," and bomb the global economy back to the dinosaur age.

PEER REVIEW

"Peer review! Peer review! Peer review!" as the activist and sometime actor Ed Begley Jr. once shrieked on a talk show. Like so many believers in the true faith of Global Warming, Begley seems to imagine that merely the mantra-like repetition of that magical phrase acts like Lord Voldemort's avada kedavra curse on all climate skeptics.

Well done!

Really?

Einstein's papers weren't subjected to peer review. (Indeed, when one journal tried to do so, he wrote back stiffly: "I see no reason to address the—in any case erroneous—comments of your anonymous expert. On the basis of this incident I prefer to publish the paper elsewhere.") Nor was Watson and Crick's landmark 1953 paper on the structure of DNA. Does this mean their science is less trustworthy than that of such multiply peer-reviewed authors as, say, Michael Mann (q.v.) or Phil Jones?

People

"The temperature was well over 100, and the air was a haze of dust and smoke. The streets seemed alive with people. People eating, people washing, people sleeping. People visiting, arguing, and screaming. People thrusting their hands through the taxi window, begging. People defecating and urinating. People clinging to buses. People herding animals. People, people, people, people."
—Paul Ehrlich describing a taxi ride in Delhi in *The Population Bomb*, 1966

Do you get the impression that Ehrlich doesn't like *people* very much?

PEOPLE FOR THE ETHICAL TREATMENT OF ANIMALS (PETA)

Scary animal rights organization whose heady brew of wild, hormonal rage, burning self-righteousness, and catwalks prove an intoxicating lure for the mostly supermodel-class teen and twenty-something females who swell its ranks.

Then, later, they grow up, get married, and realize that actually the last thing they want is for their kids to "Go Veggie" like PETA recommends ('cos how are they to get their protein?), and that actually there's nothing that sets off a crocodile-skin clutch or a nice pair of pure python Manolos than a beautiful sable coat.

PEW FOUNDATION (*See* DRAWBRIDGE EFFECT)

PHARAOHS

The era of the Pharaohs—at the tail end of the early Holocene 5,000 to 10,000 years ago—was significantly hotter than it is now. Amazingly, this managed to happen without anyone—even Pharaoh himself—driving a gas-guzzling 4 x 4 or flying in a jet, private or otherwise. It also failed to result in dramatically rising sea levels: if it had done, the Nile Delta would have been flooded to the point of uselessness and Egypt's ancient civilization could never have existed.

PLANT FOOD

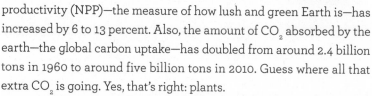

Nothing annoys Warmists more than to be told that their favorite, earth-destroying trace gas, CO_2, is in fact harmless, beneficial plant food. Except, maybe being told that all that man-made "carbon" they've been campaigning to ban these last few decades is actually *greening* the planet.

But it's true. What the satellite data shows is that since the 1980s net terrestrial primary productivity (NPP)—the measure of how lush and green Earth is—has increased by 6 to 13 percent. Also, the amount of CO_2 absorbed by the earth—the global carbon uptake—has doubled from around 2.4 billion tons in 1960 to around five billion tons in 2010. Guess where all that extra CO_2 is going. Yes, that's right: plants.

Plutonium

Deadliest substance known to man? Nowhere near—as the great physicist Dr. Bernard Cohen once offered to demonstrate on camera to anti-nuclear activist Ralph Nader. Cohen said he would eat as much pure plutonium as Nader would eat pure caffeine. Had Nader agreed, of course, he would have died while Cohen would be doing just fine.

POLAR BEAR

The most hideously endangered creature in the entire world, ever. More endangered, even, than the Dodo, the Great Auk, and the Tyrannosaurus Rex, which, though admittedly extinct, suffer the grave disadvantage of being neither photogenically white and fluffy, nor having cute little baby cubs which slide charmingly down snow banks in David Attenborough nature series about the threatened Arctic....

Since at least the 2000s (when, for no fact-based reason it was declared "threatened" under the U.S. Endangered Species Act), the polar bear has been the poster creature for The World Is Melting and It's All Our Fault movement. It has starred in *An Inconvenient Truth*; in several much-reproduced (and sometimes photoshopped) images of lonely ursines on apparently remote, melting ice floes; in an advertising campaign for Plane Stupid; in Greenpeace's Project Thin Ice fundraising drive; in a *Vanity Fair* photoshoot with Leonardo DiCaprio; and in numerous heartrending news articles—later to become a scandal known as Polarbeargate (q.v.)— about bears which allegedly drowned due to man-made global warming.

There's just one small problem with this: the polar bear is doing just fine. No, better than fine. Since the 1950s, world polar bear populations have exploded, from around 5,000 to between 20,000 and 25,000. Does a four or fivefold increase in a species' population over a period of just sixty years sound to you like it's in any kind of danger? Me neither. That sounds more like an infestation. A dangerous infestation for, let's not forget, the polar is one of the most aggressive, man-eating carnivores on the planet.

Save the polar bear? Not if we know what's good for us.

Cull the polar bear? That's more like it. Not for our sake, you understand. But for all those children of future generations who might otherwise get eaten in their beds.

POLARBEARGATE

In 2004, Charles Monnett and some fellow researchers for the U.S. Minerals Management Service were flying over Alaska's north shore when they spotted four polar bear carcasses floating in the sea.

Could this be the ultimate proof of man's selfishness, greed, and callous cruelty in allowing the planet to warm so alarmingly that yay, verily, even the very polar bears were drowning?

Well, Monnett et al. certainly seemed to think so. In a report for the journal *Polar Biology*, they extrapolated from this flimsy piece of evidence the notion that global warming was killing polar bears by increasing the frequency and intensity of summer storms and melting the bears' icy habitat. Lone females and females with cubs, they posited, would be especially at risk.

Quite a dramatic thesis to base on just four dead bears glimpsed from a light aircraft. But it was proof enough for the greenies—notably Al Gore in his *An Inconvenient Truth*—who spread the news far and wide. The polar bears were drowning! The polar bears were in danger of being wiped out due to global warming!

But were they? Not if you know anything about polar bears, no. The clue's in their Latin name Ursus maritimus—sea bear. That's because they spend an awful lot of time in the sea where they can float and swim very comfortably for hours—even days—on end. In late 2008, a radio-collared adult female polar bear in the Beaufort Sea made a continuous swim of 687 kilometers over nine days and then intermittently swam and walked on the sea ice surface an additional 1,800 kilometers.

Global warming is not going to wipe out the polar bear. They adapted to and survived a much warmer period—and more greatly reduced sea ice levels—in the previous interglacial warm period about 5,000 to 7,000 years ago.

As commenter Grizzled Bear at the website Watts Up With That? trenchantly put it: "It seems that the 4 unfortunate bears cited were destined to give their lives so that a couple of pseudo-scientists could use their deaths as part of a political statement."

POLITICS

By all means, read up on the science, but never forget that what this is really about is politics.

Environmentalism has almost nothing to do with the environment and almost everything to do with control, power, vested interests, draconian ideology, money, and, ultimately, the totalitarian urge which has possessed half the human species since time immemorial and which continues to make life so much harder than it needs to be for the rest of us.

Climate change is not a crisis which will suddenly be solved once the scientific experts know a bit more. It was never a real crisis in the first place. Think of it rather as a proxy battle zone—a bit like Angola was for the Soviets in the 1970s, or Korea was for China in the 1950s, or Afghanistan was for Iran and Pakistan in the 2000s—in a much broader ideological conflict.

In 1930s Europe, the stalwarts of the environmental movement would have made excellent fascists, Communists, or Nazis; in Revolutionary France, they would have been fervent sans-culottes; in Mao-era China they would have been Red Guards or Cultural Revolutionaries, applauding as their parents were carted off to re-education camp or execution having reported them for showing insufficient zeal on one of the chairman's fly-killing drives.

Totalitarian movements always attracts the worst sorts: the Puritans, the sociopaths, the rule-makers, the bullies, the tyrants, the petty bureaucrats, the sneaks, the thieves. Environmentalism is sadly no exception.

POPPER, KARL

Austro-British philosopher; promoter of the "falsifiable" hypothesis (1902–1994).

A scientific theory is only useful if it contains the key to its own destruction, Popper argued. That is, for a scientific proposition to be of any real value, it must be "falsifiable"—capable of being proved wrong through experiment and observation.

The classic example he gave is the proposition: "All swans are white." In order to prove this hypothesis wrong, all you need to do is find a black swan. The hypothesis has then been "falsified."

This example may sound simple to the point of obviousness, but it's essential if we're to understand a) how scientific knowledge advances, and b) how the most powerful and all-pervasive theory of our age—Anthropogenic Global Warming theory—is useless to the point of meaninglessness.

There are many cases from scientific history where widely accepted theories have been overturned—"falsified"—by evidence. One recent one is the theory that stomach ulcers are caused by stress; another is that passive smoking represents a significant health hazard.

Now let us try to apply the falsifiability test to Anthropogenic Global Warming theory.

We can't because the theory is not one theory but a bundle of theories. It embraces the idea that CO_2 has a significant warming effect on the planet; that the relatively tiny amount of CO_2 produced by humans is enough to make a big difference; that the damage done by warming outweighs the benefits; that there's an ideal global mean temperature which we should aim to keep static; that this is something we are capable of achieving; and so on.

The scientific evidence supporting this bundle of theories ranges from poor and disputed to non-existent.

But despite its many weaknesses AGW theory has one insuperable strength: it's quite impossible to prove wrong because it is incapable of falsification. As science, it is worthless. As politics, it's pure evil genius.

PORTUGAL

Birthplace of port, Vasco da Gama, and many other wonders whose names temporarily elude me.

Pity the poor Portuguese. In 2005, a former environment minister called Socrates became their prime minister on a "green jobs" ticket. Soon virtually the entire economy was being diverted to wave power, wind power, solar power, electric cars....

Portugal's economy has now tanked, while unemployment has skyrocketed and the country survives on massive bail-outs from the EU. Meanwhile, the EU continues to urge economies like Portugal's to adopt ever more stringent renewable energy policies.

Anyone know the Portuguese for "cognitive dissonance"?

POST-NORMAL SCIENCE

Should scientists lie and cheat and twist data and misrepresent evidence for the greater good?

If your answer's "No," you believe in "Normal Science."

If your answer's "Yes," you believe in "Post-Normal Science."

Post-Normal Science (PNS) was first described in the 1990s by two obscure academics—Silvio Funtowicz and U.S.-born academic and Communist Party fellow traveler Jerome Ravetz—but is now part of the intellectual mainstream. The great global warming scare could probably never have happened without it.

Here's why: in the good old days—though of course there were professional lapses—scientists saw themselves above all as seekers-after-truth. As Charles Darwin said: "A scientific man ought to have no wishes, no affections—a mere heart of stone."

Today, however, different rules apply—as you may judge from this quote from Mike Hulme, professor of Climate Change in the School of Environmental Sciences at the University of East Anglia.

"Self-evidently dangerous climate change will not emerge from a normal scientific process of truth seeking although science will gain some insights into the question if it recognises the socially contingent dimensions of a post-normal science."

Hulme at least deserves credit here for brazen honesty. What he's tacitly admitting here is that "climate change" is unlikely ever to be proved with hard evidence. It's much more akin to a convenient sociological theory invented to advance a political agenda.

"The function of climate change I suggest is not as a lower case phenomenon to be solved.... Instead, we need to see how we can use the idea of climate change—the matrix of ecological functions, power relationships, cultural discourses and material flows that climate change reveals—to rethink how we take forward our political, social and economic and personal projects over the decades to come," Hulme writes.

Few are quite so explicit about this as Hulme. But this, essentially, is how the climate scientists who have been promulgating the great global warming scare have come to justify their behavior. Science, they have persuaded themselves, ought to serve a higher purpose than mere truth—for what if the truth it reveals is the "wrong" truth? What, for example, if the evidence shows that global temperatures aren't soaring continually upwards? And what if it turns out that in ages past, global mean temperatures were warmer than the present?

To a Normal scientist of the old school there would be no dilemma here. The right answer is whatever emerges from rigorous scientific experimentation and observation.

To a Post-Normal scientist of the modern age, however, the noble lie is sometimes preferable to the inconvenient truth.

PRECAUTIONARY PRINCIPLE

Climate alarmists often tell us that even if the threat of Catastrophic Anthropogenic Global Warming is—at best—unproven, we still need to act NOW on the *precautionary principle*.

It's a neat idea. So neat, in fact, that I've made a list of other potential threats, at least as dangerous and just as plausible as CAGW, that we really must prepare for now, before it's too late.

1. Potential threat: vampire invasion—not by cute, goofy ones like in *Twilight*, but proper evil ones like in *Salem's Lot* or *30 Days of Night*. Solution: every household to be provided by the government with one bulb of garlic, one phial of holy water, one cross. (Estimated cost: $1 billion.)

2. Potential threat: asteroid collision. Solution: powerful, asteroid-smashing rockets to be installed in strategic positions all over the planet. (Estimated cost: $1.5 trillion.)

3. Problem: dolphins turn evil and enslave the world, like on that episode of *The Simpsons*. Solution: provide every household with a tank of fresh fish to appease the evil dolphins and make them return to the sea. (Estimated cost: $30 billion.)

4. Problem: a new Ice Age. Solution: dismantle every single climate action program, defund every scientist and administrator in the man-made global warming industry, shut down every solar and wind farm, scrap carbon taxes, abolish the EPA, sell everyone involved in the climate change scam as slaves to the Saudis. (Estimated cost: zilch; estimated benefits to mankind: $50 trillion.)

PRIUS

Car; twenty-first-century answer to the cilice—or hair shirt.

From early Christian times right up to the present, the cilice—or, hair shirt—has been worn by religious penitents in order to atone for their sins. Traditionally made of goatskin or coarse animal hair—sometimes enhanced with twigs or thin wires—its purpose is to irritate the skin and induce suffering as a sign of penitence. St. Thomas a Becket, the archbishop of Canterbury martyred by Henry II, owned a particularly splendid example: as his body was being prepared for burial, the lice within his cilice began to boil over "like water in a simmering cauldron."

Adherents of the modern environmental religion—a.k.a. Gaia worship—have their own version of the cilice. It's the dull, tinny, ugly, uncomfortable, pokey Toyota Prius with a track record so poor that in 2012 2.8 million older models had to be recalled by the manufacturer because of faulty steering parts and water pumps.

The main difference between the two is that whereas the cilice was designed to be worn discreetly so that no one but the sufferer would know he was wearing it, the Prius is more often driven as an act of ostentation. "See how serious I am about combating climate change," it says, as it rattles along sanctimoniously, belching wafts of righteousness and smugness from its exhaust pipe.

In 2012 the Toyota Prius was the top-selling car in California.

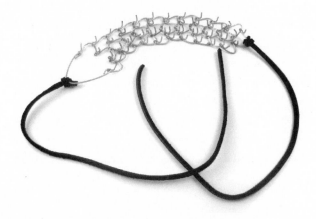

PROFIT

"Profit before planet. Who is making deals with your government?" says a leaflet I keep on my desk, a bit like how General Montgomery kept a photograph of Rommel just to remind himself of the enemy's true nature. Appropriately enough, it's from a group describing itself as FOE. That'll be the caring, nurturing campaign group Friends of the Earth, and the reason I so cherish this particular piece of literature is that it scarcely bothers even *pretending* that its goals have anything to do with environmentalism.

Its real foe is capitalism.

If you don't appreciate that anti-capitalism is what the green movement is really about, then you don't understand the green movement—or the problem.

Let's get back to first principles:

Profit is the essence of free market capitalism. Without profit there can be no motive for entrepreneurs to take the risks required to offer us all the newer, cheaper, more efficient goods and services which make our lives easier and more pleasant than ever before, and our children's lives better still. This is Western industrial civilization in action: a process of constant technological and economical progression.

For centuries profit was widely and uncontroversially accepted by businesses as their primary goal. And this wasn't—whatever bodies like FOE may think—because businesses are selfish and evil and only interested in feathering their own nests at the expense of the hapless consumer. Rather, it's because as most non-Marxists instinctively understood, the profit motive is not just economically sensible but also morally virtuous.

It is through profit that successful businesses grow and unsuccessful businesses wither. This is hard on the unsuccessful businesses but good for everyone else, for it rewards enterprise, enriches workers and shareholders, gives consumers what they want, and helps enable "scarce resources" to be allocated as efficiently as possible.

All this, however, is anathema to the Left, which is ideologically fixated to the notion that free markets are intrinsically "unfair" (true: in a system that creates winners, there will always be losers) and that this unfairness can only be rectified by government intervention.

Environmentalism is merely a fashionable cloak used to make bitter, envy-driven socialism seem urgent, reasonable, and scientifically justified. But whatever the ostensible pretext—be it saving polar bears, preventing species extinction, protecting the planet from climate change—the underlying goal remains the same: higher taxes, more regulation, more government intervention.

If you didn't know this already, green is the new red.

PROPERTY RIGHTS

> *"The moment the idea is admitted into society, that property is not as sacred as the laws of God, and that there is not a force of law and public justice to protect it, anarchy and tyranny commence."*
> —John Adams, 1787

> *"Property is the fruit of labor ... property is desirable ... is a positive good in the world. That some should be rich shows that others may become rich, and hence is just encouragement to industry and enterprise."*
> —Abraham Lincoln, 1864

Property rights are indeed one of the cornerstones of Western civilization. It is no coincidence that the modern environmentalism is so determined to remove them.

You might think your property is your own; the greenies think property is theft, and your property is really theirs—so that they can defend its true working classes, the snails and slugs, birds and bees, moths and mosquitoes who deserve to overthrow the oppressor human class. *Non-humans of the world unite! You have nothing to lose ... because you never owned anything anyway.*

QUIZ

1. In the immediate aftermath of the Boston Marathon bombings, what was *New York Times* columnist Thomas L. Friedman's preferred solution?

   a) More stringent FBI screenings of suspected terrorists

   b) A carbon tax

2. Since the 1950s, the global polar bear population has increased fivefold. Which of the following does this sound like?

   a) A species under threat

   b) A dangerous infestation

3. In 2010, a terrible fire in Israel's Golan Heights devastated 1,300 hectares of forest. Was this

   a) —as Greenpeace claimed of the fires that season—"a direct expression of the effects of climate change" and a sign that "Israel must cancel its plans to construct another coal plant, reduce use of fossil fuels, and realize that we are dealing with an international struggle"?

   b) triggered by a global warming activist at a Rainbow Festival trying to burn her used toilet paper in an attempt to be eco-friendly?

4. We are often told that 97 percent of climate scientists agree with the "consensus" on global warming. How many climate scientists were consulted to reach this figure?

   a) Oh, thousands, tens of thousands probably. They wouldn't quote a figure like that unless it were truly representative.

   b) 77 (*see* Consensus? What Consensus?)

5. When Al Gore sold his environmental TV channel Current TV for $500 million (of which he took home around $100 million), the buyer was

   a) an organic collective of nurturing tofu-weavers based in San Francisco

b) an anti-Semitic TV network—Al Jazeera—owned by the oil-rich
   state of Qatar

6. In early 2011—using the same computer models it frequently uses to
   warn of catastrophic anthropogenic global warming—Britain's leading weather forecaster, the Met Office, predicted a "barbecue summer." What happened?
   a) One of the most glorious summers in living memory, with happy
      families improving their rib sauce recipes and chargrill techniques
      every magnificently sunny weekend that God sent
   b) A total washout, offering yet further proof that the £200 million-
      a-year taxpayer-funded Met Office is quite incapable of predicting
      what the weather is going to do two months ahead, let alone over
      the next few decades

7. In 1971, the Environmental Protection Agency (EPA) conducted a
   seven-month investigation (featuring more than nine hundred pages
   of testimony) into the effects of the pesticide DDT. At the end, Judge
   William Sweeney concluded that DDT posed no health hazard either
   to man or to fish, birds, or other wildlife. Which did EPA administrator William Ruckelshaus decide?
   a) To go with evidence. Clearly, what all that expert testimony showed
      is that DDT is harmless—unless you're a mosquito—and should
      therefore be kept as a valuable weapon in the war on one of the
      world's deadliest killers, malaria.
   b) To ignore the evidence and ban DDT in the United States any-
      way—leading to several third world countries banning it, too, thus
      condemning millions of people in malaria zones to miserable,
      preventable deaths

8. Overpopulation: the elephant in the room, right?
   a) Or what! We're already at seven billion, and if this goes on much
      longer, we're going to be swamped, I tell you, swamped. It's just
      isn't sustainable. Our planet has only so much carrying capacity.

You should read Paul Ehrlich's *Population Bomb*. He saw all this stuff coming....

b) You've got to be kidding. Population growth is slowing, not accelerating. And no way is the world even close to being overcrowded. You could fit the entire current population into the state of Texas—and still the density would be no greater than in New York. The world's landmass is 732 times the size of Texas. Worried? Not.

9. Which of these people are members of the sinister, neo-Malthusian, anti-capitalist, anti-growth organizations the Club of Rome, the Club of Madrid, or the Club of Budapest?

a) The Dalai Lama, Vaclav Havel, Kofi Annan, Peter Gabriel, Bianca Jagger

b) Al Gore, Deepak Chopra, Paolo Coelho, Mikhail Gorbachev, Jimmy Carter

10. In December 2012, *USA Today* announced on its front page, "Climate change behind rise in weather disasters." This was

a) because there has indeed been a dramatic rise in extreme weather events. Call it "global weirding," call it what you will, but it ain't normal, and it's about time we did something

b) a scaremongering headline—based on a report by Munich Re, a German reinsurance company with a strong vested interest in talking up the climate change "threat"—contradicted by almost every real-world metric. U.S. tornado and hurricane activity are all down; so is flooding; so—despite the anomalous drought of 2012—are droughts; as, too, are bushfires in Australia, typhoons in China, and windstorms in Europe. Even the fervently alarmist Intergovernmental Panel on Climate Change has been forced to concede that "climate change" has not led to an increase in extreme weather events.

(The correct answers are all "b"—apart from 9, where the answer is both "a" and "b.")

RECYCLING, THE UTTER POINTLESSNESS OF

Recycling is a total waste of life.

Deep down we all know this. "I'm not against recycling…" we begin by saying. But then comes the almighty "but…."

Why are people so scared to admit it? Because, a bit like equality, communism, and multiculturalism, recycling sounds like it really ought to work if only we all close our eyes and clench our tiny fists and wish hard enough. Being against recycling is like refusing to say "I believe in

fairies" in that audience-participation moment when you go see *Peter Pan*. Do you really want to be the one responsible for the death of Tinkerbell?

Well, killing Tinkerbell may be a bit of tragic collateral damage we're going to have to accept on this one. Here's the truth: recycling is just a ritual form of self-mortification designed to make *bien-pensant* guilt-trippers feel less bad about living in a capitalist system of abundance.

Oh sure, there are a few things that *are* worth reclaiming from the trash and using again—steel, aluminium, copper, whatever—but the point about any efficient capitalist system is that stuff that should be recycled naturally is. You've seen the machine in *Toy Story 3* that strips all the trash into its constituent parts, valuable metals from worthless plastic dinosaurs, glass from cowboy rag dolls. Well, since the movie came out, those machines have got even better. Why have they got better? Because, as we say in Britain, "Where there's muck there's brass." That is, scrap metal has a value. So it attracts entrepreneurs who want to extract that value in the most efficient and profitable way possible.

But, of course, that solution is way too sensible and effective and free market for the greenies who, thanks to their Agenda 21–style (q.v.) infiltration of local government, now make the rules for our garbage disposal industry. (If only it were still run by the mafia, like in the good old days!) Instead of letting capitalism take care of the problem, they've gone for something more akin to Maoism. Just as all Chinese were expected to give freely of their time to eradicate their daily quota of flies, rats, bourgeois, capitalist-running dog lackeys, or whatever, so today in the supposedly free West we are expected to make daily obeisance to the green recycling god.

In Britain, for example, householders are now expected to sort their trash into as many as nine different color-coded bins. The system is not optional. If you refuse to play the game—or innocently forget to put the right color-coded bin out on the right day or accidentally mix your trash—you are liable either to a hefty fine or being denied the local government waste disposal service (which you, of course, have paid for with your local taxes).

Does this Nanny Statism provide any significant environmental benefit? Hardly. Much of that painstakingly recycled waste ends up being shipped to the Far East, there to be re-sifted by lowly paid trash-pickers or sent where it should have gone in the first place—to a landfill.

Research from Seattle suggests that it takes a typical household about forty-five minutes per week to recycle its rubbish. That works out, in the United States, to about ninety million man hours expended every week dividing green glass from brown glass from cardboard from aluminium from paper from plastic—to no practical purpose whatsoever.

Our precious time, it would seem, is the one ultimate scarce, non-renewable resource those greenies have no concern about squandering.

REDWOOD NATIONAL PARK

We all love the National Parks, right? Here are the human costs of the creation of just one of them—the 132,000-acre Redwood National Park—in Del Norte County, California.

Jobs lost in forestry sector on its creation in 1968: 2,757

Jobs lost in forestry sector on its expansion in 1978: 4,218

Jobs lost in forestry sector on its expansion in 1990: 900

Percentage of Del Norte County's population now out of work: more than 25 percent local poverty rate when park was founded in 1968: 5 percent

Local poverty rate by 1998: 22.9 percent

Children in Del Norte County living below the poverty line: 31 percent

National Park Service's predicted number of visitor days to Redwood National Park first fifteen years: 1.6 million

Actual, recorded number of visitor days in Redwood National Park's first fifteen years: 39,000

Predicted cost of park, as promised to U.S. Senate in 1968: less than $92 million

Actual cost of park, as of 1995: $1 billion

R

Refugees

Predicted number of "climate refugees" who, according to United Nations Environment Program in 2005 would be displaced as a result of global warming by 2010: 50 million.

Actual number of "climate refugees" displaced as a result of global warming by 2010: zero.

RENEWABLES 1

Everyone knows we need more renewable energy. How do they know? Well, because it's got "new" in it and "renew" and "able." And it involves nice, lovely, natural things like wind, which is breezy and keeps you cool on a hot day and is great when you're a kid flying a kite. Solar, too, which comes from the sun and if we can just learn to harness even a fraction of its power, why, evil, dirty, fossil fuels would be banished forever, and greed and selfishness would almost certainly be abolished with it, and we'd all live in peace and harmony under a rainbow sky. Why, to not like renewable energy, you'd have to hate nature itself....

Yeah, right.

For renewable energy to make any kind of sense whatsoever, its benefits would have to exceed its costs. This they don't, with the odd rare local exception such as Norway whose physical geography makes hydroelectric power a viable option. But that's about as far as it goes: wind; solar; biomass; tidal; and so on, are virtually useless as serious substitutes for fossil fuel (or nuclear) energy a) because they're so relatively expensive, and b) because of their dreadful side-effects ranging from environmental blight to squandering farmland and causing food riots.

Why, then, are renewables so widely believed to be the *solution*—and not, as they really are, the *problem*?

Two reasons, both equally stupid and wrong.

First, plummeting educational standards have essentially resulted in the lobotomization of the entire Western world, meaning that when a few green campaign groups blather on about "harnessing nature's free energy," hardly anyone bothers to subject this claim to the rigorous scrutiny of a cost-benefit analysis.

Second, partly as a result of reason one, we have most of us been persuaded that there are these things called "scarce resources" which we need to preserve for "future generations"—and that, as a result of this, renewable energy is both a moral and economic necessity.

In truth, renewable energy is neither of these things. Far from being moral, it represents a grotesque confidence trick on the credulous populace, perpetrated by an unholy cabal of green activists and the cynical, rent-seeking corporatists who have flocked to the subsidized renewables sector like vultures to a rotting carcass. There is nothing moral about: artificially driving up the cost of energy; enriching corporate fat cats at the expense of the poor; distorting free markets through compulsory tariffs and subsidies; trashing the countryside; driving up food prices; wiping out birds and bats; diverting land from food production to cost-ineffective energy production.

RENEWABLES 2

To supply the USA's 300 million inhabitants with energy using renewables rather than fossil fuel would require, as zoologist Matt Ridley points out in his book, *The Rational Optimist*:

> Solar panels the size of Spain, or
> Wind farms the size of Kazakhstan, or
> Woodland the size of India and Pakistan, or
> Hydroelectric dams with catchments one third larger than all the continents put together.

R

REVELLE, ROGER

Oceanographer (1909–1991) doomed to be remembered by history mainly as the Harvard professor who first alerted the young Al Gore to the threat of "Climate Change."

Poor Dr. Revelle—another tragic victim of the curse of Gore. In *An Inconvenient Truth*, Gore set up his old professor as the Godfather of Global Warming. Yet, in truth, Revelle would have utterly deplored the vast, expensive junk-science industry which has arisen, partly as a result of Gore's prostitution of his good name.

He said as much, in a paper he co-wrote shortly before his death. "The scientific base for greenhouse warming is too uncertain to justify drastic action at this time."

Gore's response? To put about the rumor that Revelle was sick and not in his right mind and had been coerced into writing it by co-authors in the pay of the fossil fuel industry. He even tried to leak this story to ABC presenter Ted Koppel.

Koppel was unimpressed: "The measure of good science is neither the politics of the scientists nor the people with whom the scientist associates. It is the immersion of the hypothesis into the acid of truth. That's the hard way to do it, but it's the only way that works."

Rio Earth Summit (1992)

Where the craziness began: ground zero for the great, global "Climate Change" panic.

ROAD TO HELL, THE

".... is paved with good intentions." One of the dangers of the green movement is that, taken at face value, the legislation it demands at first seems so reasonable and desirable. Only later does its hidden menace become clear—as Senator Howard Baker noted in 2009 in this speech to the Senate on the subject of the Snail Darter (q.v.).

Mr. President, the awful beast is back. The Tennessee snail darter, the bane of my existence, the nemesis of my golden years, the bold perverter of the Endangered Species Act is back.

He is still insisting that the Tellico Dam on the Little Tennessee River, a dam that is now 99% complete, be destroyed.

In the midst of a national energy crisis, the snail darter demands that we scuttle a project that would produce 200 million kilowatt hours of hydroelectric power and save an estimated 15 million gallons of oil.

Although other residences have been found in which he can thrive serenely, the snail darter stubbornly insists on keeping this particular stretch of the Little Tennessee River as his principal domicile....

Let me stress again, Mr. President, that this is fine with me. I have nothing personal against the snail darter. He seems to be quite a nice little fish, as fish go.

Now seriously Mr. President, the snail darter has become an unfortunate example of environmental extremism, and this kind of extremism, if rewarded and allowed to persist, will spell the doom to the environmental protection movement in this country more surely and more quickly than anything else....

We who voted for the Endangered Species Act with the honest intentions of protecting such glories of nature as the wolf, the eagle, and other treasures have found that extremists with wholly different motives are using this noble act for meanly obstructive ends....

Surprise, surprise ...

ROMM, JOE (*See also* ANGRY)

Blogger.

Comedy villain—like Skeletor in *He-Man and the Masters of the Universe*, only without the winning charm, arch-critic of climate skeptics—whom he regularly accuses of being "anti-science" and "deniers" "in the pay of Big Oil"—almost certainly invented by an evil genius in the pay of the Koch Brothers in order to discredit the cause of climate alarmism. A bit rich, you might say, coming from a man so nakedly in the pay of Big Soros.

ROYAL SOCIETY FOR THE PROTECTION OF BIRDS (RSPB)

Britain's leading ornithological organization and Europe's biggest conservation charity, founded in 1889, originally as a protest group campaigning against the use of exotic bird feathers in women's hats. For years, RSPB was assumed to stand for Royal Society for the Protection of Birds. However, its recent tireless advocacy on behalf of the wind industry suggests it may be due for an official name change: Royal Society for the *Prevention* of Birds.

SANTA CLAUS (*See* GREEN JOBS)

SATELLITE DATA

This consistently shows less
"global warming" than the surface
temperature data— especially after those
surface temperature records have either been
lost by organizations such as the Climatic Research Unit or
"adjusted" by experts like Dr. James Hansen.

Which do you think is the more likely explanation?

a) Stupid satellites. What do they know?

b) The surface temperature records are untrustworthy for a number
of reasons, ranging from the urban heat island effect and the reduction
in the number of weather stations to the highly politicized tinkerings
of the activist scientists in charge of keeping and analyzing these
records.

SCARES

Global warming is bird flu is acid rain is swine flu is the ozone layer is
the Millennium Bug is the 1970s ice age panic.... Once you've anato-
mized one scare, you realize they follow the same trajectory. Here, as
described by Christopher Booker and Richard North in
Scared to Death, are the key stages:

1. Scientists come up with the idea that some
   genuine problem is caused by something
   else that in fact has nothing to do with it.

2. The media pick up the scare, hyping it up
   without questioning the science—using the
   scientists to give it a seeming plausibility.

3. The politicians get carried along by the scare.

4. Politicians introduce incredibly damaging regulations to deal with the supposed problem. But, at the same time, truth begins to emerge that the scare was not justified and that the regulations are misplaced.

5. The scare itself dies away, but the misconceived regulation stays in place doing damage for years to come.

SCHNEIDER, STEPHEN

Arch-warmist; IPCC lead author, professor of Environmental Biology and Global Change at Stanford University (1945–2010).

Few scientists have fought to keep the great global warming scam going with quite such vigour as the late Stephen Schneider. Yet, as this revealing quotation from a *Discover* magazine interview suggests, he was under few illusions about the paucity of evidence supporting the alarmist narrative.

"On the one hand as scientists we are ethically bound to the scientific method, in effect promising to tell the truth, the whole truth and nothing but—which means that we must include all the doubts, caveats, ifs and buts. On the other hand, we are not just scientists but human beings as well. And like most people we'd like to see the world a better place, which in this context translates into our working to reduce the risk of potentially disastrous climate change. To do that we need to capture some broad-based support, to capture the public's imagination. That of course entails getting loads of media coverage. So we have to offer up scary scenarios, make simplified, overdramatic statements and make little mention of any doubts we might have."

This is Post-Normal Science: the belief that scientists have a responsibility to a cause even higher than truth; that their job is not merely to observe and record data but to act as moral arbiters too, even if it means taking short cuts—or abandoning the rigor of the scientific method altogether—in order to achieve the *right*, or rather, Left, political ends. That's neither noble nor scientific … nor right.

SCIENTIFIC METHOD, THE

How do we know that the moon is not made of green cheese? Can we be sure that Al Gore is not a pustulous, slime-breeding Reptulan from the Crab Nebula, third cousin five times removed to Jabba the Hutt? Is our planet on the verge of being destroyed by Catastrophic man-made Global Warming (CAGW)?

The solution to all these vexed questions of our time is to be found in the Scientific Method— the process of elimination by which we acquire knowledge about the natural world and sift the true from the untrue.

If you look it up on *Wikipedia,* you will find its origins traced to a tenth-century Arab scholar called Ibn al-Haytham. This may be true. But it may equally be one of those patronizing politically correct memes—a bit like the one which ascribes the invention of "zero" to Islam, even though, in fact, it was invented centuries earlier—devised by white liberal academics to make non-Western cultures feel better about themselves. Either way, it is not a question that can be resolved by the Scientific Method, for it is a matter of opinion not testable fact.

In its simplest form, the Scientific Method comprises five stages: question; hypothesis; prediction; test; analysis.

Let's apply it to Al Gore, shall we?

Clearly, we would need to test our hypothesis with a series of experiments. A good start might be to sneak up behind him while he was standing on his podium at one of his $100,000-a-gig speaker events, grab his hair, and pull very hard. If his human mask came off to reveal a scaly, lizard-like head underneath, it would certainly go some way to confirming our theory that he was a Reptulan.

But if it didn't, it would by no means signify that our hypothesis had been "falsified." It would simply mean that further experiments were necessary. Perhaps, we simply hadn't pulled at his hair hard enough. Maybe we pulled in the wrong place. Who knows? The only solution is to try again and again until that particular "test" had been found wanting.

Quite possibly, the only truly effective test would be to extract his DNA sample and compare it with that of a real human being. Perhaps this could be achieved surreptitiously by slipping a masseuse into his hotel suite and distracting him. Anyway, you get the general idea.

As to those other questions we mentioned at the beginning. The green cheese one is easy: we've been to the moon and found it is in fact made of rocks and stuff, not cheese, green or otherwise.

The man-made global warming one, however, is much trickier. This is not because it is technically more complex than any other technically complex scientific question of our time. Rather, it's because the cabal of scientists who have appointed themselves the gatekeepers of truth on this particular subject appear to have decided that in this case the scientific method need not apply.

We're constantly being told that global warming is about "the science." In fact, it's anything but about "the science." If it was about the science, we'd be hearing a lot more about why global warming stopped in 1997.

As to the question of whether Al Gore is a pustulous, slime-breeding Reptulan from the Crab Nebula, the jury is still out. But that shouldn't stop us experimenting. Indeed, I firmly believe that as human beings it is our bounden, nay, holy duty to defend our planet and our species by putting his identity to the test at every opportunity.

"SCIENTISTS"

"Scientists say carbon emissions are too high to stop climate change." "Scientists say Hurricane Sandy likely linked to record Arctic Sea loss this year." "Climate change threatens French truffle, scientists say." "Aliens may destroy humanity to protect other civilisations, say scientists."

Scientists. Is there *anything* they don't know?" Well, no, obviously not. That's why they appear on your television, in your newspaper, and on your radio, pretty much every day, issuing dire prognostications about the terrible future which undoubtedly awaits us for the crime of daring to exist. Because they just *know. Everything.* It's why they're called "scientists." From the Latin "scientia"—meaning "knowledge." But, of course, if you're a scientist you knew that already.

In the old days, "scientist" was merely a general term used to differentiate people who cultivated the sciences (mathematics, physics, chemistry, natural history, etc.) from those who inclined towards the arts (music, painting, poetry, and so on).

Today, however, the word has acquired a much more nuanced meaning: Guardian of the Bunsen-Burning Flame of Wisdom; Dispassionate Seeker-After-Truth; White-Coated Seer Who Knows All and Sees All; Selfless, Immeasurably Noble, Scrupulously Neutral Arbiter of All That Is Right and True Not Only in the Realm of Science But in All Other Fields Besides; Experts' Expert at Everything That Requires Expertise.

How did this happen? Did scientists become much cleverer? Did the bar for a Ph.D. get suddenly raised so much higher?

Not exactly. Not at all in fact. What happened was the discovery that "science" could be used by political activists as a handy excuse to advance their agenda under the guise of studied objectivity. "Hey, it's not because we're a bunch of crypto-Marxist control freaks that we're demanding higher taxes, more regulation, and the replacement of Western industrial civilization with a Soviet-style global command economy run by leftist technocrats. It's because the science tells us that that's what we need to do."

So next time Al Gore appears at a lecture hall near you, you know what to do. Our safety and our future may depend on it.

SEA LEVEL RISES

What alarmists say:

Sea level rises predicted by Al Gore in the "near future" in *An Inconvenient Truth*: twenty feet.

> *"It is now clear there are going to be
> massive flooding disasters around the world."*
> —Dr. David Vaughan, British Antarctic Survey, 2009

> *"Sea levels to rise by more than 1 metre by 2100"*
> —headline report from 2012 Doha Climate Conference

What the real world data says:

Sea level has been rising since the end of the last ice age. Based on tide gauge data, the generally accepted rise is 1.5 millimeters per year. There has been no recent acceleration. Recent satellite data suggests that between 2002 and 2007 the sea level actually fell. Coral islands like the Maldives, far from being inundated by climate change, are actually increasing in size because coral is a living thing.

Another green myth scuppered by reality.

SEUSS, DR.

Learned doctor who posited in his influential 1971 text *The Lorax* the thesis that deforestation, unchecked economic growth, and resource depletion can lead to serious environmental damage.

Critics, however, have noted that Dr. Seuss's paper was not peer-reviewed—and even if it had been still remains vastly inferior to his two earlier scientific studies of delinquent feline behavior. There have even been suggestions that Seuss was a pseudonym and that his doctorate may have been faked.

SHALE GAS

As garlic is to vampires, so shale gas is to greenies: an affront to their entire belief system.

Why do greenies—such as Matt Damon, Yoko Ono, and Susan Sarandon—hate shale gas so? Let us count the ways.

It's abundant across the world. In the United States alone, there is enough to provide at least one hundred years' worth of energy at current usage.

1. It's cheap. In the United States, thanks to shale, the price of natural gas has more than halved, meaning lower fuel prices for both business and consumers.

2. It's carbon-friendly. Of all the world's major economies, America's is the only one to have experienced a significant drop in CO_2 emissions (by 12 percent) since 2007—despite the fact that the economy has grown (albeit slowly) in that period. This is almost totally the result not of renewables but of the rapid replacement of dirtier energy sources such as coal and oil with shale gas.

3. It improves energy security, breaking the dominance of Russia and the Middle East in natural gas. America has already felt the benefits, turning from a net importer to a net exporter of natural gas in less than a decade.

4. It's safe. Despite overcooked horror stories—earthquakes, water table pollution, methane in faucets—put about by the alarmists' well-funded propaganda industry, shale gas has an industry record considerably more eco-friendly than, say, wind power.

Can you see why these truths might prove somewhat inconvenient to a green movement which would like to persuade us that all fossil fuels are a) scarce, b) increasingly expensive, c) carbon-unfriendly, d) vulnerable to energy security issues, and e) dangerous?

SHARKS

There are worse ways to
go, no doubt, than death
by shark—death by being
eaten alive by fire ants, maybe;
death by a thousand cuts; death by
being subjected to repeated viewings of Al Gore's *An Inconvenient
Truth*—but we can surely all agree, not many.

It's those layers of serrated, triangular teeth; the fin cutting through
the water; the cold, dead eyes; the gaping jaws; the prehistoric killing-
machine efficiency: each one of these facets speaks to our deepest,
primeval fear. The fear of being eaten alive by a savage beastie with
nasty, pointy teeth.

Anyway, I mention this because I was in western Australia, recently,
just after it had acquired the dubious distinction of becoming shark
attack capital of the world. There had been five fatalities in eleven
months (that's a lot: as many as the International Shark Attack files tells
us we should expect in the entire world in a year), and what bothered
me most (apart from having to glance over my shoulder every few
seconds every time I went swimming) was the apparent lack of witch-
hunt frenzy.

Just for the record, if I ever get "taken" by a shark—or a crocodile or
a snake or whatever creature it is, even if it's a cute kitten with one blue
eye and one orange eye and a pretty red ribbon round its neck—I want
the perpetrator of my death hunted down and destroyed. What I do not
want—as seems to have become worryingly the custom with animal
attacks on humans these days—is to have well-meaning friends and
relatives saying: "It was just an animal following its natural instincts.
James wouldn't have sought revenge on an innocent creature." Yes,
actually, James would.

What kind of weird, warped world do we now live in when—for
perhaps the first time in the existence of the human race—we have
become so intellectually decadent that we've come almost to accept
animal attacks on humans as the natural order of things?

S

One of the phrases you often hear after shark attacks, for example, is, "Well, of course, what do we expect when we trespass in their domain?"

Excuse me? Hello? Whatever happened to the idea of God giving man dominion over all of His creation? Who made this new rule that when you're in the sea, sharks get a free pass to eat you because it's their territory not yours? Since when did a cold-blooded, prehistoric fish—whose species could never even manage to type a John Grisham novel with its ventral fins, let alone the works of Shakespeare—acquire rights equivalent to those of humans?

Which isn't to say I'm so shark-phobic I want them all turned into soup for the Chinese. I recognize that the world would be a poorer place without them: there'd be no *Jaws*—*I*, *II*, or *III*; there'd be no cage-diving vacations to come back from and impress your friends with; and I guess we'd all miss that frisson of trepidation you get any time you step into the water in Florida, California, South Africa, or Australia.

But what I am saying is that having rightfully worried once about hunting sharks to near extinction, we've now allowed the balance to go too far the other way—as we have done with so many of our traditional enemies from wolves and bears to crocodiles and snakes.

I've no doubt if Tyrannosaurus rex were still stalking the earth, we'd be busily trying to appease him, too. "Well of course, he can hardly be blamed for wiping out that entire kindergarten class at the Dino Park. His species got here before we did. We are mere interlopers in his domain...."

It's not just the eco-loons who hold this kind of view. It's gone mainstream. It's the norm.

And if that kind of pussy liberal, surrender-monkey intellectual decadence is the way we're going, then frankly, we deserve all the eating we get.

Silent Spring

"Without this book, the environmental movement might have been long delayed or never have developed at all," wrote Al Gore in his foreword to a reprint of Rachel Carson's 1962 bestseller.

So: another of those "imagine if we could go back in time and assassinate Hitler" fantasy scenarios, then. Certainly, many more people would be alive today—standards of living would likely be higher, too—if this infernal book had never been written.

Still, Gore was right about one thing. *Silent Spring* set out the road map for modern environmentalism: radical, counterproductive action inspired by public hysteria based on junk-science.

The brilliant title was Carson's editor's idea. (Carson had been going to call it *Man Against the Earth* or *The War Against Nature*.) It envisaged a future in which, apart from various cancer epidemics, birdsong would never again be heard due to reproductive problems caused by wanton use of pesticides. In fact, the research she quoted—by Dr. James DeWitt of the U.S. Fish and Wildlife Service—showed the complete opposite of what she claimed it did. Pheasants fed high doses of DDT (q.v.) actually hatched *more* eggs, not fewer.

Yet five decades on, *Silent Spring* continues to play an important role in environmentalist propaganda and fundraising, as well as in shaping policy. All on the basis of exaggerations, distortions, and flat-out lies.

SIMON, JULIAN

Libertarian economist; nicknamed "the Doomslayer" thanks to his ruthless demolition of the spurious claims made by neo-Malthusian catastrophists such as Paul Ehrlich; Cornucopian; inspiration for Bjorn Lomborg's *The Skeptical Environmentalist***; (1932–1998).**

No, the world is *not* going to hell in a handcart due to man's rabbit-like reproduction and wanton consumption of scarce resources. On the contrary, things are getting better all the time. Thanks to his brilliant ingenuity, man is the solution *not* the problem.

For this counterintuitive view, Simon was mocked by many and admired by a discerning few as a "Cornucopian"—kind of a more intellectual version of Forrest Gump. Simon himself baulked at the term: it made him sound like a naïve optimist rather than the hard-headed data-miner he actually was. Though Simon started out as a "card-carrying anti-growth, anti-population zealot," he changed his mind when he realized that the evidence told otherwise.

The facts of life, he discovered, really are conservative.

SIMPSON, HOMER

Safety inspector at the Springfield Nuclear Power Plant, widely understood by all television viewers, except campaigners from the green movement, to be a satirical, yellow cartoon character rather than a real person.

Skeptics

*"Perhaps we should stop accepting the term 'skeptic.'
Skepticism implies doubts about a plausible proposition.
Current global warming alarm hardly represents a plausible proposition. Twenty years of repetition and escalation
of claims does not make it more plausible. Quite the contrary, the failure to improve the case over 20 years makes
the case even less plausible as does the evidence from
Climategate and other instances of overt cheating."*
—Dr. Richard Lindzen, professor of Atmospheric Physics, MIT

SKYROCKET

*"Under my cap and trade system,
electricity prices would necessarily skyrocket."*
—Barack Obama, January 2008

In this respect at least, the president has been true to his promise. Cap
and trade may have failed, but thanks to "green" tariffs and the EPA's
war on coal, the cost of energy has risen faster than inflation; the only
thing restraining energy prices is the shale oil and gas boom of which
Obama is the unwitting beneficiary.

SNAIL DARTER

Before the Northern Spotted Owl, before the Texas sand dune lizard,
before the Polar Bear, there was the snail darter. All right, so it was just
a crappy little fish, about the size of two paper clips end to end, which
you couldn't catch, you couldn't eat, you could barely even see. But this
was the 1970s, and they had to start somewhere.

And so it was that, for a few heady years between 1973 and 1979, this
two-bit, no-consequence, pug-ugly three inches of mud-hugging,

bug-eyed piscine slime would find itself promoted by the greenies into the most important, cherishable, and oh-so-to-be-preserved-at-all-costs species in the whole wide world.

The pretext for this promotion was the construction of the Telico Dam on the Little Tennessee River. An environmental activist professor at the University of Tennessee wanted the dam stopped, and the snail darter was his perfect excuse. Apparently—or so the enterprising prof claimed—the dam would ensure the destruction of this magnificent fish, which no one had heard of 'til ten minutes ago when the prof discovered it on a speculative snorkeling expedition. So the new Endangered Species Act was invoked, and the $140 million dam project was put on hold, while the Tennessee legislators wrangled over which would prevail: human progress or a tiny fish.

Only by the skin of its teeth did progress win. The dam project, though almost complete, was very nearly nixed till a dramatic intervention by Senator Howard Baker (*see* Road to Hell, The).

Meanwhile, the snail darter lives happily on in its new home on the nearby Hiwassee River in Tennessee. Predictions of its extinction, it seemed, had been somewhat overdone. Spotted owls, polar bears, anyone?

SNOW

Formerly (2001): tragic harbinger of man-made climate change whose imminent disappearance will make our world all the poorer. (See, for instance, the headline from *The Independent*: "Soon children will have forgotten what snow looks like," or the UN IPCC 2001 report: "Milder winter temperatures will decrease heavy snowstorms.")

Currently: Deadly and terrifying white nightmare which we can expect to see more and more of, as incontrovertible proof of man-made climate change.

(See, for instance, the headline in in the *Guardian*, December 2010: "That snow outside is what global warming looks like.")

SOLAR CYCLES (*See* YEAR(S) WITHOUT A SUMMER)

SOROS, GEORGE

Dr. Evil.

Actually, that's not fair. George Soros is way, WAY more evil than Austin Powers's lovable nemesis. And with tentacles in every pie, too, as we see from his unlikely presence in a book on Eco-Fascism.

But can it really be that in between running his Manchurian Candidate Barack Obama, picking off sovereign currencies with the random yet clinical mercilessness of the Beltway Sniper and radically destabilizing the global economy, the Dark Lord can yet find time in his busy schedule for green issues as well?

Why, most certainly! Indeed, it is a principal part of the plan he outlined in his not-unscarily titled 1993 book, *Towards a New World Order*, and later in *The New Paradigm for Financial Markets: The Credit Crisis of 2008 and What It Means*. The old free market business model is dead, Soros believes. (Or claims to believe.) What we need now, he argues, is a new paradigm where green business becomes the "motor of the world economy."

Sound familiar? It should: you've heard often enough from the likes of Barack Obama and David Cameron about these wonderful "green jobs" which are magically going to lift us out of the Great Recession. But where do you think our leaders got the bright idea for such mighty success stories as Solyndra, the biofuel industry, and all those other economic miracles which have made us all so much richer, happier, and freer?

Here's a clue, from a 2008 Bloomberg report: "Obama has endorsed much of a Center for American Progress plan to create 'green jobs' linked to alleviating global climate change."

And guess who funds the Center for American Progress to the tune of $27 million year—including the shrillest, most aggressive, and hysterical climate alarmist blog of all—Joe Romm's Climate Progress?

And guess whose Foundation in 2006 shamelessly listed a $720,000 grant spent on "politicization of science"—and which stepped into help fund a case by one James Hansen after his employer NASA tried to gag him from making so many embarrassing statements about global warming?

And guess who handed $3.1 million to the hard-left Tides Foundation, which, in turn, finances such extremist environmental activist groups as Sea Shepherds, Earth First!, and the Ruckus Society?

With facts like these—and bear in mind, these represent just a fraction of the money the billionaire Soros spends every year financing climate change alarmism—who needs conspiracy theories?

Now obviously, when you're on a mission to save the world from a threat as deadly as global warming, you need some recompense for your selflessness. And, by uncanny coincidence, many of Soros's most lucrative business interests elide happily with the cause of climate-change alarmism.

In 2007, Soros invested $900 million to help replace some of that pesky Brazilian rainforest with planet-saving biofuel plantations. In 2009, he pumped $1 billion into so-called "Clean Energy" projects. In 2011, he teamed up with one of Obama's "Energy Czars" Cathy Zoi and the $14 billion private equity firm Silver Lake to launch yet another green fund.

What a pity it would be if, despite all these noble efforts, economic and scientific reality were to triumph over all that expensively bought propaganda and the bottom were to fall out of the Climate Change market! Poor George Soros. However would he manage to scrape together his next billion?

Specialists

"An open society (that is, a society based on the idea of not merely tolerating dissenting opinions but respecting them) and a democracy (that is, a form of government devoted to the protection of an open society) cannot flourish if science becomes the exclusive possession of a closed group of specialists."
—Philosopher Karl Popper

SPECIES LOSS (*See* EXTINCTION RATE)

SPERM COUNT

Sperm counts are falling across the world. It's because of all the estrogen in the water supply from our wanton use of birth-control pills. Or chemicals or pesticides or plastics or something. Pretty soon, things are going to get so bad that we'll be forced to use sex for recreational purposes only and do all our breeding in laboratories like something out of *Brave New World*. Apparently.

Except it's all nonsense. The meme originated in a 1992 paper in the *British Medical Journal*, claiming that sperm counts had fallen by 50 percent in fifty years. Despite its weak documentation, it was subsequently cited in more than 1,000 scientific papers: no wonder so many people believe it.

However, a more recent fifteen-year study in Denmark found "no indication that semen quality has changed."

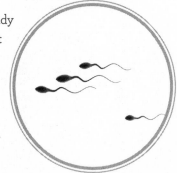

All that has really changed is that the number of mamby-pamby, greenie metrosexuals has increased and made women think sperm counts have fallen.

What the world needs now is more manly right-wing men. But, then again, you knew that.

SPLATTERGATE (*See* NO PRESSURE)

SPOTTED OWL

"Endangered" fantasy creature, dreamed up by green campaigners in order to close down the forestry industry in the American West. Arguably the most successful—and ecologically and economically destructive—campaign in the history of modern environmentalism.

If the Northern Spotted Owl didn't exist, the environmental movement would have had to invent it. Actually, scrub that: the environmental movement DID invent it for the Spotted Owl they campaigned for at their protest rallies, in newspaper columns, on television, and in Washington had very little to do with any avian species known to ornithologists.

The Northern Spotted Owl of environmentalist myth is a delicate, highly sensitive creature, forever teetering on the brink of human-induced destruction. This is because, besides being close to extinction, it is also incredibly fussy: apparently, in order to survive, each breeding pair requires many thousands of acres of old-growth forest. (New-growth forest just won't do.) Hence the ecologists' argument that in order to save the Spotted Owl, the forestry industry in the Pacific North West had to be destroyed.

As a result of the noisy and sometimes violent 1990s Northern Spotted Owl campaign, twenty-four million acres of old growth forest are now no-go areas for the loggers. An estimated 50,000 jobs have been killed in the milling and logging industry, and for every forestry job lost, five more are lost in ancillary industries. So that means around 250,000 livelihoods ruined to save the Spotted Owl.

Still, at least an endangered species has been preserved, right? Well, maybe. Depends on how threatened you believe the owl was in the first place. The theory that the Spotted Owl can only survive in old-growth forest derives from three studies from just one biologist, Eric Forsman. Yet, two years after the ban, more than eleven thousand spotted owls were counted—many nesting in precisely the kind of locations environmentalists said they couldn't survive in: second-growth forests and clear-cuts.

To this day, no link between old-growth harvesting and declining owl populations has ever been established. (A more likely culprit, it seems, is predation from the Barred Owl.) What's certain is that the effect on the human populations in the forest counties of states such as Washington, Oregon, and Montana has been devastating. In those counties, incomes have dropped, jobs are scarce, services are declining, school rolls are falling. Oh, and the forests are in worse shape, too, because "protection" means no one is allowed to clear the underbrush nor thin out the trees, leading to less healthy stock and the constant threat of devastating fires.

Stern, Nicholas (See also STERN REVIEW)

Dreary English civil servant—specializing in development economics—promoted well above his pay grade after discovering the magic formula of man-made global warming. Thanks to his *Stern Review* (q.v.) Sir Nicholas—later Lord—Stern became arguably the most terrifyingly influential ex-dreary civil servant in the history of the world.

STERN REVIEW

It took twenty-three UK treasury economists and officials (led by Sir Nicholas—now Lord—Stern) sixteen months and £1.27 million to produce the 700-page *Stern Review of the Economics of Climate Change.* Quite a lot of time, money, and effort for a report now widely acknowledged as a pile of junk.

Unfortunately, that's not how the political class greeted its recommendation that at least one percent of global GDP needed to be diverted to fight the war on Climate Change. Tony Blair, prime minister at the time, hailed it as "the most important report on the future ever published by this government." In the IPCC's Fourth Assessment Report, it was cited no fewer than twenty-six times in twelve different chapters as expert confirmation of the economic case for "combatting climate change."

The economists who have assessed it since know otherwise. Their principle criticism is that when calculating the costs of action or inaction on climate change, Stern uses an improbably low discount rate. A discount rate is the cost of doing something now versus the benefit accrued in the future.

Stern's *Review* ignores that "future generations" are, if our economies are not derailed by the greenies, going to be richer than our own thanks to technological progress. So, it'll be easier for them to deal with any adverse effects of climate change, whether that means building flood barriers or desalination plants—or subterranean shopping malls to protect us from the next Ice Age.

What Stern is asking us to do—in the midst of an economic crisis deeper and longer lasting than the Great Depression—is that for no solid scientific reason we take a hit on behalf of people who will be richer than we are. If a future Bill Gates came knocking at your door, insisting you handed over one percent of your income this year and every year so as to help him maintain the solar panels by his swimming pool, you'd surely tell him where to shove it.

Pity our political class weren't similarly frank with Nicholas Stern.

Strong, Maurice

Marxist billionaire who organized the Rio Earth Summit; promoter of sustainability, rule by an enlightened environmentalist elite, and the New World Order; world's most dangerous Canadian.

SUNOCO/SUN OIL (*See* DRAWBRIDGE EFFECT)

SUPERSTITION

We live in an age where writers such as Richard Dawkins and Christopher Hitchens are hailed as clear-eyed prophets, while practicing Christians are dismissed by the cognoscenti as deluded fools who worship a "Big Sky Fairy." We congratulate ourselves that we have moved beyond the dogma and foolishness of organized religion into a new age of enlightened, science-based rationalism.

But this isn't how future generations will judge us. On the contrary, they will find little to choose between the superstitions and empty rituals of the Western world's fastest-growing new religion: Gaia-worship—or environmentalism—and of those credulous ages past where men sacrificed captured prisoners to the sun god, or read omens in the behaviour of celestial bodies, or purchased indulgences to buy time off purgatory in the afterlife.

We ravage our landscape with wind turbines not because there is the slightest evidence that they are remotely beneficial, but rather as a potent and easily recognizable symbol of our commitment to the green cause (*see* [Bat-Splatting, Bird-Slicing] Eco-Crucifixes).

We painstakingly divide our household waste between a growing number of colored eco-bins, less because recycling has a net environmental benefit—it mostly doesn't—than as a daily act of ritual obeisance.

We treat those who express any form of scepticism about the new religion not as free thinkers with a perfectly valid point of view but as heretics to be reviled, shunned, and cast into outer darkness.

We allow our existence increasingly to be regulated by an array of powerful religious authorities—the IPCC, the United Nations, the EPA—whose directives have the force of holy writ.

We listen, rapt, to the doomy prognostications and fire-and-brimstone sermons of the high priests of our religion—Al Gore, Rajendra Pachauri, the Prince of Wales, etc. And when their personal standards of self-abnegation fall somewhat short of the hair-shirt lifestyles they seek to impose on the rest of us, we shrug our shoulders and say that their noble motives justify their lives of self-indulgence.

We indoctrinate our children with the view that the natural world, rather than something to be enjoyed and celebrated (how medieval, how "Merrie England!"), should be viewed through a filter of guilt and shame, for man is not the pinnacle of creation but the threat to all creation.

We frighten our children into "correct" behavior with terrifying stories of the awful things that will come to pass if they err from the true path.

We persuade ourselves that if we're too weak to practice self-denial, we can remit our sins simply by the act purchasing indulgences—in the form of carbon credits, carbon offsets, eco-friendly detergents.

We pepper our landscape with hideous turbines—not because they do any good: they don't—but because the bat-chomping, bird-slicing eco-crucifixes mark the progress of the holy green empire.

SUSTAINABILITY

Mmm. Sustainability. It sounds so nice, doesn't it? So earthy and chunky-knit and wholesome and nourishing.

Sustain, like an extended note on a shepherd's pastoral flute.

Sustain like sustenance: a hearty lentil stew after a brisk stomp across the moors on a crisp winter's day.

Sustain like one of Sting's twenty-four-hour tantric orgasms....

Yes, whoever chose that innocent, pleasant-seeming word to represent one of the most pernicious and insidious political doctrines of our age chose it well. For, what kind of cynical, greedy, ruthless, cigar-chomping, kitten-drowning, life-loathing scumbag would you have to be to be against something as self-evidently good as sustainability?

The kind of scumbag who understands what it really means, I guess.

Sustainability in environmentalese has nothing whatsoever to do with flutes, or lentil stew, or chunky sweaters or even—blessed relief—Sting's prolonged tantric sexual acrobatics.

Rather, it is a codeword for rationing, wealth-redistribution, deliberately engineered economic stagnation, and the wholesale global adoption of eco-fascist values, ultimately enforced by One World Government.

Sound extreme? Well, here's Maurice Strong, making no bones about what it means, in his role as secretary-general of the United Nations Conference on Environment and Development:

"Current lifestyles and consumption patterns of the affluent middle class—involving high meat intake, use of fossil fuels, appliances, home and work-place air-conditioning and suburban housing—are not sustainable. A shift is necessary which will require a vast strengthening of the multilateral system, including the United Nations."

Sustainable Development

An oxymoron. Development means progress, technological advancement, and rising living standards. Sustainability—in an environmentalist context: see above—means the exact opposite.

The phrase entered popular currency in 1987 with a report called *Our Common Future*, produced by a commission headed by the then-prime minister of Norway, Gro Harlem Brundtlandt. As you would expect of a concept born of Scandi-socialism, sustainable development is really just egalitarianism and global wealth redistribution with a fashionable green tinge.

Just occasionally in the report, the mask slips.

"Painful choices have to be made," it says.

Why? And by whom?

SUZUKI, DAVID

Canada's Al Gore.

"Money isn't what matters," Canada's leading environmental campaigner told a newspaper in October 2012. And to prove it, just a week earlier, this selfless crusader had asked for a modest stipend of only $30,000 for delivering a speech to 1,600 high school kids at Canada's John Abbott College, Quebec. The speech was titled: "The Challenges of the 21st Century: Setting the Real Bottomline." Possibly not all that different from one he'd delivered at a naturopath convention three years earlier, titled, "The Challenge of the 21st Century: Setting the Bottom Line." But that's the great thing about serious environmentalists: they really believe in recycling.

So great are the risks the heroic Dr. Suzuki takes on his mission to save the world that he sometimes requires bodyguards. Young, female ones for preference, like the college students he requested via an assistant on his visit to John Abbott College.

"Why females you ask? Well, he is a male. No seriously, I believe it is his way of being discrete [sic] and less intimidating," explained one college administrator to another via email while discussing Dr. Suzuki's unusual request.

Discretion and non-intimidation. Does this kindly man's generosity and consideration know no bounds? (Hat tip to Donna Laframboise and Ezra Levant.)

S

TESLA

"You can't polish a turd" goes the old music industry saying. Apparently, no one mentioned this to the celebrities lining up to buy California's electric super-car.

Teslas look great. Teslas look shiny. Teslas look as sleek and sexy and racy as any petrol-driven sports car you ever saw.

Problem is, the Tesla is only as good as its battery-powered engine, which, in turn, is only as good as the charge it can store. So, if you're planning a journey any longer than eighty or so miles and you haven't got a day to spare waiting for it to be recharged—in the unlikely event, that is, that you can find a specialist station capable of recharging it—then you'd be quicker taking the bus. Or walking.

The Tesla, in other words, is the green motor industry's equivalent of a Potemkin Village.

"You have seen the future—and it works," it says. "Here is a car which allows you to feel smug, eco-friendly, and righteous—but without the inconvenience of having to make any adjustments to your greedy, selfish, capitalist lifestyle."

Except it's not the future. It's more like a return to the eighteenth century when long journeys were a luxury for the rich and where you couldn't go any distance without having to break up your journey in a succession of flea-bitten coaching inns. I thought it was a DeLorean you needed for that kind of reverse time travel....

T

THATCHER, MARGARET

Britain's greatest peacetime prime minister; the Gipper's wing-woman in the war against the Evil Empire; alleged Cassandra of "global warming."

When Baroness Thatcher died, about the only kind thing the Left could find to say was to hail her as a green heroine for having recognized, earlier than any other major political leader, the urgency of the global warming "problem."

Sadly, this terrible slur contains an element of truth. The key moment was a speech she gave in 1988 in the City of London, which went like this:

"For generations, we have assumed that the efforts of mankind would leave the fundamental equilibrium of the world's systems and atmosphere stable. But it is possible that with all these enormous changes (population, agricultural, use of fossil fuels) concentrated into such a short period of time, we have unwittingly begun a massive experiment with the system of this planet itself."

What, of course, this claim neglects to mention is the dramatic change of heart she had later in life, once she realized how badly she'd been conned on this issue by her advisors. In her 2003 book *Statecraft*, in a passage entitled "Hot Air and Global Warming," she wrote:

"The doomsters' favourite subject today is climate change. This has a number of attractions for them. First, the science is extremely obscure so they cannot easily be proved wrong. Second, we all have ideas about the weather: traditionally, the English on first acquaintance talk of little else. Third, since clearly no plan to alter climate could be considered on anything but a global scale, it provides a marvellous excuse for worldwide, supra-national socialism."

As she once famously said: "This lady is not for turning." Except, it would seem, on the issues that really mattered.

THE NATURE CONSERVANCY (TNC)

Though only the world's tenth biggest NGO, The Nature Conservancy is a strong contender for number one most dangerous. The reason for this is that, in the innocent guise of saving the environment by buying up tracts of land and preserving them for posterity, it has amassed for itself so much money, influence, and unaccountable power.

Headquartered in a $28 million, eight-story office building in Arlington, Virginia, TNC controls more than one hundred million acres of land. In late 2008, these assets were valued at $6 billion and contain trillions of dollars worth of natural resources which can now never be used for anyone's benefit again—except with TNC's permission.

Like a medieval monarch, TNC increases its influence by dispensing favors to the nation's rich and powerful from Hollywood to Wall Street, from the big corporations and law firms to the Pentagon and the seats of academe. These favors range from greenwashing by association (many of TNC's most generous donors also happen to be America's biggest polluters) to selling on particularly beautiful stretches of land at generous discounts under its questionable "conservation buyer" program.

Here, according to investigative journalist Elizabeth Nickson, is how it works: "A TNC member or staff identifies a desirable piece of property. TNC purchases that property, often at a discount because it is a land preservation charity, and the owner of the property receives a tax write-down from the appraised value of the land. TNC then strips the land of development rights, that is, the right to cover that land with industrial waste, trailers, tract homes, strip malls, and so on. It then sells the land on to a private owner at a discount. The new owner can build a house, cabin, stables, septic system, dock, etc., but (generally) can't develop the land as anything but an estate.... The new owner [often a board member or member of TNC] then donates the difference in the price of the land, if developable, between its maximum and the price he paid to TNC, receiving a tax write-down of the original amount. Everybody wins, except the taxpayer." And, as with most green schemes, the wealthy green elite get to enjoy the land—and you don't.

"THINK GLOBALLY, ACT LOCALLY"

Just so you know, the guy—Rene Dubos—who devised this immensely tedious, fatuous, right-on green mantra back in the 1970s, later recanted his enviro-loon ways. "Nature does not know best," declared Dubos, dismissing the romantic notion that, freed from man's pernicious influence, the natural world is benign and lovely and self-healing. There is nothing wrong with man adapting the world to his changing needs, argued Dubos, provided he does so in a spirit of "noblesse oblige"— mindful of his role of nature's guardian. The greenies never forgave him.

TIMES ATLAS OF THE WORLD

Yet another once great institution hijacked by climate alarmists. In 2011, the *Times Atlas of the World*—first published in 1895—threw over a century's tradition and distinction out of the window by apparently abandoning cartographical rigor for environmental activism. For its latest edition, it hit on the bright idea of showing Greenland not as it currently is—but as it *might* look once "climate change" has taken its toll. This involved shaving 15 percent off its ice cover over twelve years—far greater than the ice melt observed in that period by glaciologists. An *Atlas* spokeswoman was unrepentant. "We are the best there is," she said.

TOWELS

Time we struck back. I do it through the medium of towels. More specifically, towels in those hotels where there's a prissy sign lecturing you on how rare and precious water is and urging you to save the planet by putting your towels back on the rail rather than on the floor, to signal that you don't require the towels to be washed.

Excuse me? When I checked in at reception, did I *ask* for my *en suite* bathroom to come complete with a sanctimonious environmentalist homily? Am I supposed, somehow, to be grateful or impressed that the hotel is exploiting the vogue for all things green in order to save itself some money? Isn't the whole point of paying to stay in a ritzy hotel that you get clean sheets, clean towels on demand at any time of day or night? Isn't that part of the fun?

Just say no to "No clean towels." I do, every time.

TOY STORY 3
(*See* RECYCLING, THE UTTER POINTLESSNESS OF)

TROLL

Internet slang for someone who comes to a website in order to disrupt, distract, sabotage, or annoy; especially prevalent below climate skeptic websites.

Below my own climate skeptical blog in the *Telegraph,* I keep a magnificent menagerie of trolls. Some specialize in saying, repeatedly, how shocked they are that a "once-serious newspaper" is prepared to publish such "unutterable rubbish"; others in referring readers to climate alarmist stories they have seen reportedly uncritically at the *Guardian*, Grist, Salon, or Real Climate; others in attacking my physical appearance, my educational background, my history of depressive illness, my performances on TV or radio, my style, my sense of humor....

Here's the weird thing though: what these people almost never ever do is actually engage with the facts and logic of the argument I've presented. Now, why would that be, I wonder?

When you're taking flak, it means you're over the target. This is why I take such pleasure in the Orcish hordes of malevolent trolls who come to stalk my climate-skeptical blog posts: their inarticulate rage, their cheap-shot ad homs, the poverty of their counter-arguments remind me daily of just how comprehensively we skeptics are winning the debate.

TURNER, TED

Cable TV owner, America's biggest individual private landowner, environmental activist.

"A total world population of 250–300 million people, a 95 per cent decline from present levels, would be ideal," he told an interviewer with *Audubon* magazine in 1996.

So when the great cull finally comes, are Turner's five children and their descendents going to be included in this? Or do different rules apply when you're a rich, caring environmentalist like Ted?

TWITTER FEED, PAUL EHRLICH'S

A brief guide to the charm, wit, and understatement of climate expert and MacArthur Genius prizewinner Paul Ehrlich, as shown by his Twitter feed:

#Climate disruption. Remember this when denier morons claim snow proves no warming. Just the opposite. #greed. http://bit.ly/Xiwu7G

#Overpopulation and idiocy—more on the *WSJ*'s latest moron. Right wing struggling to find even dumber "analysts," http://bit.ly/WxTdva.

#Climate disruption. Arizona pol gives more evidence we'll never run out of morons, http://bit.ly/XfuVW9.

Friends of Fraud—#Republithugs on the rampage #plutocracy, #greed, http://nyti.ms/UkMJTb.

Tricky Dick pioneering the techniques of todays #Republithug, #plutocrats. Richard Nixon's Even-Darker Legacy, http://readersupportednews.org/opinion2/277-75/15846-richard-nixons-even-darker-legacy.

WSJ gibbing idiocy on #population, http://on.wsj.com/Ytfg6p, no accident. Part of Murdoch empire's attempt to murder our grandkids for profit.

#Population. Julian Simon proved by example long ago the ultimate resource, which will never be exhausted, is morons, http://on.wsj.com/VBAmmd.

Words of genius, no?

UNITED NATIONS

Glorified and highly expensive, New York–based talking shop designed to help Third World kleptocracies, obscure island states, Islamofascist dictatorships, and banana republics get over their sense of grievance and inferiority.

If only those were the limits of its ambitions. Unfortunately, it also sees itself as a future One World Government—as witness its increasingly all-encompassing, supranational environmental regulatory bodies. The Intergovernmental Panel on Climate Change itself is a UN construct—born out of three UN organizations: the World Meteorological Organization, the International Council of Scientific Unions, and the United Nations Environment Program. By 2004, the UN was known to have initiated more than 60,000 environmental projects. And guess who is paying for all these measures to steal your democratic rights, redistribute your income, trample on your freedoms, and regulate your existence? You.

Never on their list of what is "Unsustainable" (q.v.) is "bossy, gas-emitting, international bureaucrats growing fat at the public trough."

UNIVERSITY OF EAST ANGLIA (UEA) (AKA "UNIVERSITY OF EASY ACCESS")

University in the flat, boggy fenland of eastern England, best known for its Climatic Research Unit and its renowned Creative Writing department.

As the Climategate emails made clear, there is fierce competition between the two faculties as to which can produce the most lurid and imaginative fiction.

U

UNSUSTAINABLE

"The following are considered unsustainable by the sustainability army [of activists, conservation bureaucrats, green NGO officers]: Single-family homes, paved roads, ski runs, golf courses, dams, fences, paddocks, pastures, plowing of land, grazing of livestock, fish ponds, fisheries, scuba diving, sewers, drain systems, pipelines, fertilizer and wall and floor tiles."
—Elizabeth Nickson in *Eco-Fascists: How Radical Conservationists Are Destroying Our Natural Heritage*

Useful Innocents

"Useful innocents" was a phrase of the economist Ludwig von Mises, used originally to describe "confused and misguided sympathizers" of the Soviet Union.

It applies just as well to fellow travelers of the modern environmental movement—not the hardcore activists but all those ordinary people occupying the reasonable, middle ground whose naivety, complacency, and lack of curiosity about what being "green" really means has enabled what should have been a freaky cult at the margins of society to become part of the mainstream.

We're all guilty. Well, actually I'm not. But a lot of people we know definitely played a part in this. Maybe—admit it—even you.

U

VICTIMHOOD

Liberal terror weapon, brilliantly deployed in the wake of Climategate by more-sinned-against-than-sinning (yeah, right) climate scientists.

Open letter released six months after the Climategate scandal broke—and signed by 255 members of the National Academy of Sciences, among them Paul Ehrlich and Stephen Schneider:

"We are deeply disturbed by the recent escalation of political assaults on scientists in general and on climate scientists in particular," it begins. Having invoked such names as Galileo, Pasteur, Darwin, and Einstein, the letter concludes by calling for an end to "McCarthy-like threats of criminal prosecution against our colleagues based on innuendo and guilt by association, the harassment of scientists by politicians seeking distractions to avoid taking action, and the outright lies being spread about them."

Do you see what's going on here? Not only are the disgraced Climategate scientists being elevated to the ranks of some of most important, original, and influential thinkers in history, but they are being recast as tragically misunderstood, cruelly abused martyrs of a harsh, ignorant world quite incapable of comprehending their true scientific genius.

Really? These were the guys, remember, who were caught red-handed in a series of emails lying, bullying, cheating, abusing the scientific method, "losing" raw data, and deliberately breaching Freedom of Information laws, all while snaffling grants—courtesy of you and me: the taxpayer—running into millions of dollars.

VINER, DAVID

Obscure climate change researcher from the University of East Anglia's Climatic Research Unit propelled to international fame thanks to his prediction in the *Independent* newspaper (in March 2000), that "children just aren't going to know what snow

is." Winter snowfall, Dr. Viner predicted, would soon become a "rare and exciting event." Though now, of course, subsequent large snowfalls are also offered as evidence of "global warming" or "climate change." Funny, isn't it, how climate changes practically every day and especially between winter, spring, summer, and fall?

VIRUS

"We need to radically and intelligently reduce human populations to fewer than one billion.... Cutting a body of cancer requires radical and invasive therapy, and therefore, curing the biosphere of the human virus will also require a radical and invasive approach."
—Paul Watson, Sea Shepherd Conservation Society, star of Animal Planet's *Whale Wars*, showing yet again how truly kind and caring greenies are

"In the event that I am reincarnated, I would like to return as a deadly virus, in order to contribute something to solve overpopulation."
—Prince Philip, Duke of Edinburgh, in his foreword to *If I Were an Animal* (1986), showing that even right-wing aristocrats can get it wrong in their desire to have fewer peasants around despoiling the landscape, frightening the horses, and polluting exotic hunting grounds

VOLUNTARY HUMAN EXTINCTION MOVEMENT (VHEMT)

Environmental movement calling for all people to abstain from reproduction to cause the gradual voluntary extinction of mankind;

V

founded in 1991 by U.S. activist Les U. Knight (not his real name); estimated current worldwide membership: 400; but, hey, let's not mock: in the early days people said the Nazi Party would never catch on, either.

"If you haven't given voluntary human extinction much thought before, the idea of a world with no people in it may seem strange. But if you give it a chance, I think you might agree that the extinction of Homo sapiens would mean survival for millions, if not billions of Earth-dwelling species.... Phasing out the human race will solve every problem on earth, social and environmental." —from *Wild Earth*, vol. 1, no. 2 (Summer 1991)

Well, I guess when you put it like that, the logic is inescapable.

WAGER

In 1980, Julian Simon (q.v.) made a famous wager with Paul Ehrlich (q.v.). Who would turn out to have the better grasp of economic reality: the "doomslaying" optimist or the neo-Malthusian pessimist?

Simon invited Ehrlich to choose any five commodities. (He picked chromium, copper, nickel, tin, and tungsten.) After ten years, either Simon or Ehrlich would pay out according to whether the commodities' inflation-adjusted price had risen or fallen.

Ehrlich bet that the prices would rise, reflecting the demands of a growing population and the approaching depletion point of "scarce resources."

Simon bet that they would fall.

Ten years later, Ehrlich paid out $576.07 to settle the wager. He had been wrong on every count.

What's more interesting than the result of the bet, though, is the postscript. Ehrlich went from strength to strength, winning a MacArthur Genius Award (currently worth a cool $500,000), enjoying tenured professorships and a lucrative career as a lecturer and all-around environmentalist expert. Simon, on the other hand, spent the rest of his life being vilified as a rabidly right-wing, dangerous contrarian at war with nature and reality.

It's what they call the Reverse Cassandra Effect: in environmentalism, the rewards for being wrong are far greater than the paltry sums for being right.

WARMERGATE

Mark Steyn's preferred name for Climategate (q.v.). It's funnier—and closer to Watergate, obviously. Unfortunately, Steyn was just that little bit too late. By the time he coined it, the rival term had already gone viral and Climategate's future was assured.

WATERMELONS

Green on the outside, red on the inside. Also title of brilliant book (is there any other kind?) by one James Delingpole.

After the fall of the Berlin Wall, many disaffected leftists transferred their allegiance to the green movement as a new way of bringing down the capitalist system. Naughty lefties: Marx (q.v.) and Engels would not have approved.

WATTS UP WITH THAT? (*See also* BLOGOSPHERE)

The world's most popular climate skeptical website—guaranteed to make Michael Mann choke on his Pop-Tarts every day of the week....

"WE DIDN'T LISTEN!" (*See also* MANBEARPIG)

Catchphrase from the classic South Park episode "Two Days Before the Day After Tomorrow." "Global warming" finally comes to South Park causing mass panic, looting, stampedes, tramplings, cannibalism, and desperate attempts to flee the implacable approaching menace.

The running gag, of course, is that the panic has no basis whatsoever: the global warming menace that has descended on South Park, Colorado, and the rest of the United States exists entirely in the panicked citizens' heads.

It was first aired in 2005—four years before Climategate and the failed Copenhagen climate conference. Which just goes to show, if you want to know the facts about climate change don't go to the IPCC, go to Matt Stone and Trey Parker.

WE KNOW WHERE YOU LIVE

From Greenpeace's Climate Rescue blog, April 2010, by "Gene from Greenpeace, India":

If you're one of those who have spent their lives undermining progressive climate legislation, bankrolling junk science, fueling spurious debates around false solutions, and cattle-prodding, democratically elected governments into submission, then hear this:

We know who you are. We know where you live. We know where you work.

And we be many, but you be few.

WEATHER

Want to know the difference between "weather" and "climate"? It's really very simple. If it's cold when the greenies say it should be warming, it's weather. If, on the other hand, it's doing anything that bears any correlation with their computer models' predictions of environmental doom, then it definitely counts as climate.

WHALE WARS

Animal rights pornography for hard-core eco-fascists in which misanthropic thug Paul Watson sails round the world in his boat *Sea Shepherd*, oozing a trail of such sanctimonious guff, tedium, and blubbery hatefulness that he actually makes Japanese and Norwegian whalers look like lovable innocents in sore need of our sympathy and protection.

"WHAT IF WE CREATE A BETTER WORLD FOR NOTHING?" (*See also* PASCAL'S WAGER)

Ineffably smug and dishonest *USA Today* cartoon, much-circulated among greenies who've never heard of something called "Cost Benefit Analysis."

WHITEWASH (*See* CLIMATEGATE INQUIRIES)

WHY DIDN'T WE LISTEN?

> *"Over 4.5 Billion people could die from*
> *Global Warming-related causes by 2012."*
> —March 2007 headline in the *Canadian*—
> "Canada's new socially progressive and cross-cultural
> national newspaper"

WIKIPEDIA

For once the teachers are right: don't trust *Wikipedia*. It tries to play down the extent and significance of the Medieval Warm Period (with the help of a chart that looks suspiciously like Michael Mann's Hockey Stick); it stubbornly brands "Climategate" the "Climatic Research Unit email controversy"—taking pains, of course, to stress irrelevantly that "the scientific consensus that global warming is occurring as a result of human activity remained unchanged throughout the investigations"; and it does love to trawl up any old dirt it can find on scientists of a skeptical disposition, like Fred Singer: "[He] is best known for his denial of the health risks of passive smoking."

Wikipedia's persistent and outrageous bias was traced by Lawrence Solomon in the *National Post* to a cabal of fanatical warmists who had gained administrator status, enabling them to doctor *Wikipedia* entries to suit their political agenda. Worst of these, by far, was British Green party activist—and close friend of the Climategate scientists— William Connolley. On one of his blog posts, Connolley crowed, "A few snippets from *Wikipedia*.... I'm now an admin, and hence have

ultimate power to CRUSH ALL MY ENEMIES HA HA HA HA!!!"
Read the separate entry on Connolley, William. You'll see he wasn't
joking.

Wilderness

*"We must make this an insecure and inhospitable place for
capitalists and their projects. ... We must reclaim the roads
and the plowed land, halt dam construction, tear down exist-
ing dams, free shackled rivers and return to wilderness millions of tens of millions of acres of presently settled land."*
—Dave Foreman, founder of Earth First!
and the Wildlands Network

WILDLANDS PROJECT

I don't know about you but when I make my first few million—perhaps
as a result of the massive sales of *The Little Green Book of Eco-
Fascism*—I'm going to settle down and buy me a little piece of the
country dream. You know the kind of thing: wooden homestead with a
verandah to hang my hammock; the burbling brook, or maybe even
river to catch salmon and trout in; the well to draw my water from; the
lake to keep my sixty-foot Riva on; the 8,000 or so acres where I'll keep
my private herd of buffalo; the racetrack for my Ferrari collection; the
shack accommodation for my staff.... Nothing too fancy, you understand.

But while the details may vary, the impulse is surely common to most
of us: this deep nostalgic yearning one day to return to the wildlands
whence we all originated, there to enjoy a life of prelapsarian pastoral
bliss on the shores of our very own Walden Pond.

Except, our chances of doing so are becoming increasingly slim. I
don't mean the economy—though of course there's that, too. What I
mean is that the time is fast coming when there'll be none of that country
idyll available—not for love nor money. And if you don't believe me,

check out one of the scariest things you'll ever see on the internet: the Wildlands Project map of America.

What the map shows is how the United States will look once it has been divided up into the conservation zones environmentalists insist are necessary in order to protect "biodiversity." The map is color-coded: tiny black areas for human settlements; vast swaths of red, orange, and yellow to represent land which, to a greater or lesser degree, is barred to human activity.

It sounds like something out of Alex Jones's darkest, paranoid fantasy about the New World Order rampaging across private property rights in the United States and beyond. Except it's not a fantasy. That map—with its decreasingly tiny stretches of land not yet permanently under the control of Big Government—is the face of America's very near future.

By 2005, 473,653,970 million acres—20 percent of the U.S. land mass—was already under no-use or limited-use restrictions.

By 2010, that figure had risen to 700 million acres. In other words, one third of the U.S. land base of 2.3 billion acres is now under the permanent control of environmentalist brownshirts.

Often this state land-grab has been achieved without any need to consult—let alone compensate—the affected property owners. Their rights can be stripped at the stroke of a bureaucrat's pen: once the area has been designated a wetland under EPA regulation, earmarked as a bird conservation area by the National Audubon Society, or marked as a rare species zone by the Natural Heritage Program, the Nature

Conservancy, or the Department of Environmental Conservation, then they might just as well kiss it goodbye. What used to be their land now belongs to the red-legged frog. Or the cactus ferruginous pygmy owl. Or the desert tortoise. Or the Texas sand lizard....

Then, of course, there are the private land trusts—ninety-three in New York State alone—searching ceaselessly for new territory to acquire in order to place it forever beyond the reach of little people like you and me. In our glorious new eco-fascist future, only the chosen ones—the Ted Turners and Robert Redfords—will be granted their own private Idahos. For the rest of us, it's goodbye forever to our country dreams: quite simply, we are not worthy!

WIND FARMS, ALL THE ARGUMENTS FOR ...

Um ...

WIND FARMS, SOME OF THE ARGUMENTS AGAINST ...

They despoil the countryside and ruin the views.

They decimate rare bird and bat populations.

They are hazardous to health.

They require millions of tons of concrete, which can never be removed, to be deposited in rural locations.

They provide almost no electricity.

They destabilize the grid.

They interfere with radar.

They require thousands of miles of unsightly cabling and pylons.

They require thousands of tons of rare earth metals, imported from Mongolia, where the environment is poisoned to obtain them.

They require 100 percent backup from conventional power generation, which increases cost.

Their output is intermittent, they do not produce on demand.

They are prohibitively expensive.

They require large sums of money to be paid to landowners, at the expense of the poor, which amounts to upwards redistribution of wealth.

Their existence causes deep divisions among communities.

They drive unemployment, destroying jobs, not creating them.

Mostly they have to be imported, from countries like China.

They are an affront to the free market, surviving only as government-subsidized green boondoggles.

They have a negative impact on the tourism industry.

Wind Park; Wind Project; Wind Resource Area (WRA)

Cozy euphemisms used by the wind industry to make bat-splatting, bird-slicing, landscape-destroying, sleep-ravaging eco-death factories sound nice.

WINTER

In his essay collection *Winter*, the Canadian author Adam Gopnik reflects on how our cultural attitudes to the season have shifted over the centuries. What he makes clear is that the idea of winter as a pleasurable phenomenon—ice skating, snowy landscapes, chestnuts roasting on an open fire, etc.—is a relatively recent one. For most of mankind's time on earth, winter has been a season to be dreaded, for the nights are longer, food is scarcer, and, of course, it's uncomfortably cold.

What changed? The arrival of cheap energy, of course. In Britain, for example, you can actually see this shift in attitudes occurring in the space of less than half a century by studying two wintry poems, one from 1747 by Dr. Johnson called "Winter Walk," the other, William Cooper's 1785

poem "The Winter Evening." In the first, winter is presented as something forbidding and "horrid." By the time of the second, the author depicts a recognizably modern scene of a man sitting reading his newspaper by the fire with his coffee, delightfully removed from the bitter chill outside.

The thing that made the difference is, of course, the thing that greenies despise: the arrival of Industrial Revolution. For the first time, coal was being mined on an industrial scale, which had the knock-on effect of bringing down the price of wood so that everyone—even dirt poor people—could suddenly afford to heat their homes instead of freezing to death in noble, carbon-neutral penury.

Ain't technology a bitch, greenies?

WIRTH, TIM

Former Democrat senator for Colorado; served in the Clinton administration, working with climate hysteric Al Gore; now on UN Foundation where he lobbies for hundreds of billions of U.S. taxpayer dollars to be spent helping underdeveloped countries fight "climate change."

Two quotes sum up Tim Wirth. The first comes from his speech to the Rio Earth Summit:

"We have got to ride the global warming issue. Even if the theory of global warming is wrong, we will be doing the right thing in terms of economic policy and environmental policy."

The second is from a PBS documentary in which he boasted of how he helped rig the 1988 congressional hearing, at which a visibly sweating Dr. James Hansen famously (and dishonestly) testified before the international media, that "the earth is warmer in 1988 than at any time in the history of instrumental measurements."

"What we did is that we went in the night before and opened all the windows inside the room...so that the air-conditioning wasn't working...so when the hearing occurred there wasn't only bliss which is television cameras in double figures, but it was really hot."

WOLVES

War and Peace; *The Three Little Pigs*; *Little Red Riding Hood*; *The Howling*: What do all these stories have in common?

Yep. That's right. In every one of them—a bit like Englishmen in Hollywood action thrillers—the wolf's job is to play the bad guy.

Now, why do you think this is?

a) because throughout history man has feared and loathed the wolf, which has threatened his children, savaged his livestock, and rent the night air with its terrible, blood-curdling howling?

b) because until the modern age of enlightenment the world was filled with ignorant lupophobes who outrageously and unfairly maligned this cute, cuddly, loveable creature which wants nothing more than to be our friend and has never eaten little pigs, or grandmas, or children, not ever?

If your answer's b), congratulations: there's a healthy, lucrative future for you in the ecology industry, perhaps running one of those wonderful "rewilding" projects like they have in Yellowstone Park. You know, the one which is trashing the local elk population and destroying the livelihoods of all the neighborhood ranchers whose livestock are being killed, hamstrung, or rendered near worthless because of stress-induced weight-loss: all thanks to the campaigners who hit on the bright idea of reintroducing wolves to the region.

Like so many environmentalist ideas, rewilding North America and Europe with wolves sounds wonderful in theory but has been a disaster in practice. Why? Because wolves, being wolves, don't play by the rules. They don't know that their job is to stay in the specially designated reserves maintaining the ecological balance as top predator, while always remembering to look picturesque and proud on nature documentaries. What they want is easy meat—and they find that not in the wild but safely in pens near human habitation, where they can maul and gorge at their leisure.

The last wolf in England was killed during the reign of Henry VII; in the United States, the wolf was eradicated from most states after a nine-year campaign beginning in 1915. Was this really because they were all so much less educated back in the day? Or, was it maybe because they were considerably less naïve and stupid?

X-RATED

An excerpt from *Return to Almora*—a novel by Dr. Rajendra Pachauri (q.v.), head of the IPCC (q.v.). If you're squeamish, please look away NOW....

"She removed her gown, slipped off her nightie and slid under the quilt on his bed.... Sanjay put his arms around her and kissed her, first with quick caresses and then the kisses becoming longer and more passionate. May slipped his clothes off one by one, removing her lips from his for no more than a second or two.

Afterwards she held him close. 'Sanjay I've learned something for the first time today. You are absolutely superb after meditation. Why don't we make love every time immediately after you have meditated.'"

XXX-RATED

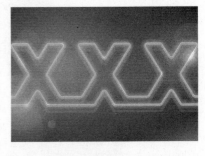

In October 2006, an Oregon masseuse claims to have been fondled and groped in a Portland hotel suite by a tipsy and octopus-like Al Gore, who appears to have expected rather more from his massage treatment than a vigorous back rub. While this has absolutely nothing whatsoever to do with climate change or environmentalism, it nevertheless strikes us as quite, quite wrong in a book of this nature not to include an excerpt from the transcript of her interview with the Portland Police Bureau.

"And he came over to where I was while I was trying to pack up and then he wrapped me in an inescapable embrace as I turned around, giving me this 'come hither' look deep into my eyes and caressed my back and buttocks and breasts. I squirmed to try and get out of his grasp, telling him to stop, don't, several times and I finally told him and said, 'You're being a crazed sex poodle,' hoping that he'd realize how weird he was being yet he persisted."

YEAR(S) WITHOUT A SUMMER

Have you ever wished you could recapture the bracing white misery of a Brueghel winter hunting scene, squint into the thrilling Turneresque sunsets which followed the Year Without a Summer, or die of hypothermia just like they used to in the good old days of the Little Ice Age?

Well, the good news is, we'll soon have no choice. A new ice age is coming. It won't be like the one some scientists and the media briefly predicted in the 1970s before changing their mind and deciding that global warming was the bigger threat—but it'll last the rest of your life and beyond. Great, isn't it? And all because of solar cycles.

Solar output goes in eleven-year cycles, with high numbers of sunspots seen at their peak. Our current cycle, Cycle 24, is showing the weakest solar activity since 1906, but the one really to worry about is Cycle 25.

Cycle 25 is predicted to be as weak as—or weaker than—the Dalton Minimum (1790 to 1830), when average temperatures in parts of Europe fell by as much as 2 degrees Celsius. If we're really unlucky, it could even be as bad as the Maunder Minimum (1645 to 1715) when those frost fairs were held on the Thames and the canals of Holland froze solid.

So brush up on those skating skills: winter is coming!

"YOU DIDN'T HUNT FOR THE MISSING CHILDREN"

When the current global warming non-crisis blows over—and it will—do you think any credit will be given to the minority of people who were right by the majority of people who were wrong?

Let me explain why it won't using my friend Gary's "You didn't hunt for the missing children" analogy.

For many years now, a large body of concerned citizens (scientists, teachers, politicians, businesspeople, environment correspondents, local government officials....) have been engaged in a frantic and increasingly desperate search for the missing children.

"What? You mean these two, sleeping here, soundly in their beds?" one or two dissenting voices have asked.

But the searchers have ignored these dissenting voices, as well they might. After all, with an issue as important and urgent as missing children, you can't allow yourself to be waylaid by distracting details. What matters is the cause, the quest! You must find those missing kids before it's too late—because if you don't, well just imagine what horrors might ensue.

The missing kids might be lost in the woods and die of exposure or be attacked by wild beasts.

The missing kids might be kidnapped—or worse—by some unsavory adult.

The missing kids might be trapped in a cave by an incoming tide or stuck down a hole or a disused mineshaft or God knows what else.

That's why it's so important that every possible resource is dedicated to this vital mission to find the missing kids.

Eventually, though, the searchers are forced to give up. They have searched the fields and rivers and woods and caves and abandoned mine shafts and pedophile basements high and low, but the kids are nowhere to be found. Wearied and despairing, the searchers return home to where the missing children are sleeping safely in their beds— as they were all along.

"They're here!" says one of the searchers, joyously.

"Yes. Just like we said," says one of the dissenting voices.

The searcher ignores the dissenting voice and turns to one of his fellow searchers.

"The kids are here. Isn't this fantastic?" he asks.

"Not really," says one of the dissenting voices, grouchily. "If you'd listened to us instead of embarking on this panicked wild goose chase you could have saved everyone an awful lot of time, money, and worry."

The searchers turn on the dissenting voice and give him a look of utter contempt.

"We're not talking to you," one of them says.

"What? Because I was right and you were wrong."

"That's got nothing to do with anything," says one of the searchers. "We're not talking to you because you're a really bad person. There we were, all last night, all of us—all the decent, caring people, that is— tearing our hair out with worry about the fate of those poor kids. We searched high and low. Our feet are sore, our legs are tired, we didn't get a wink of sleep. And what were you doing all that time? You were sat at home, watching TV with the cat on your lap and a drink by your side, not giving a toss about where those kids might be or what terrible things might have happened to them."

"But …," the dissenting voice starts to explain.

"God, you're not talking to one of those missing children deniers are you?" says another searcher, bursting into the room.

"Trying not to," says the searcher.

"Good, well it seems we've got another problem on our hands. We've found the kids but now it's the cat. No one's seen the cat for ages and if we don't find it soon there's no knowing what might happen to it. You'd better come. We need all the help we can get."

"Do you mean…," says the dissenting voice, gesturing to the cat which has been purring on his lap all this time.

"You keep out of this one, you bastard," says one of the searchers, as he hurries out of the room. "You didn't care about the missing children, so you're hardly going to be the sort who gives a damn about the missing cat…."

Z

As in Zzzzzz—a list of things caused by global warming (as noted by John Brignell at http://www.numberwatch.co.uk/).

Afghan Poppies Destroyed

Africa in Conflict

Africa Devastated

African Aid Threatened

African Holocaust

Aged Deaths

Aggressive Weeds

Agulhas Current

AIDS

Air France Crash

Air Pockets

Air Pressure Changes

Airport Farewells Virtual

Airport Malaria

Al Qaeda and Taliban Being Helped

Alaskan Towns Slowly Destroyed

Algal Blooms

Allergy Increase

Allergy Season Longer

Alligators in the Thames

Amazon a Desert

American Dream End

Amphibians Breeding Earlier (or Not)

Anaphylactic Reactions to Bee Stings

Ancient Forests Dramatically Changed

Animals Head for the Hills

Animals Shrink

Antarctic Grass Flourishes

Antarctic Ice Shrinks

Antarctic Sea Life at Risk

Anxiety Treatment

Archaeological Sites Threatened

Arctic in Bloom

Arctic Bogs Melt

Arctic Ice Free

Arctic Ice Melt Faster

Arctic Lakes Disappear

Arctic Tundra Lost

Arctic Warming (Not)

Asteroid Strike Risk

Asthma

Atlantic Less Salty

Atlantic More Salty

Atmospheric Circulation
Modified

Attack of the Killer Jellyfish

Avalanches Increased

Avalanches Reduced

Baghdad Snow

Bahrain under Water

Bananas Grow

Barbarization

Bats Decline

Beef Shortage

Beer Better

Beer and Bread Prices to Soar

Beer Worse

Bet for $10,000

Big Melt Faster

Billion Homeless

Billion-Dollar Research
Projects

Billions of Deaths

Billions Face Risk

Bird Populations Dying

Bird Strikes

Bird Visitors Drop

Birds Confused

Birds Decline (Wales)

Birds Driven North

Birds Face Longer Migrations

Birds on Long Migrations
Threatened

Birds Return Early

Birds Shrink (Australia)

Birds Shrink (USA)

Bittern Boom Ends

Black Hawk Down

Blackbirds Stop Singing

Blackbirds Threatened

Blizzards

Blood Contaminated

Blue Mussels Return

Bluetongue

Borders Redrawn

Brains Shrink

Brewers Droop

Bridge Collapse (Minneapolis)

Britain Siberian

Britain's Bananas

British Monsoon

Brothels Struggle

Brown Ireland

Z

Bubonic Plague

Buddhist Temple Threatened

Building Collapse

Building Season Extension

Bushfires

Butterflies Move North

Butterflies Reeling

Butterfly Saved

Cambodian Sex Trade Fueled

Camel Deaths

Cancer

Cancer Deaths in England

Cannibalism

Carbon Crimes

Caribou Decline

Cataracts

Caterpillar Biomass Shift

Cats More Amorous

Cave Paintings Threatened

Chagas Disease

Childhood Insomnia

Children's Mental Health

Chocolate Shortage

Cholera

Circumcision in Decline

Cirrus Disappearance

Civil Unrest

Cloud Increase

Clownfish Get Lost

Coast Beauty Spots Lost

Cockroach Migration

Cod Go South

Coffee Berry Borer

Coffee Berry Disease

Coffee Threatened

Cold Climate Creatures
   Survive

Cold Spells

Cold Spells (Australia)

Cold Wave (India)

Cold Weather (World)

Cold Winters

Colder Waters (Long Island)

Computer Models

Conferences

Conflict

Conflict with Russia

Consumers Foot the Bill

Coral Bleaching

Coral Fish Suffer

Coral Reefs Dying

Coral Reefs Grow

Coral Reefs Shrink

Coral Reefs Twilight

Cost of Trillions

Cougar Attacks

Crabgrass Menace

Cradle of Civilization
  Threatened

Creatures Move Uphill

Crime Increase

Crocodile Sex

Crocodiles Driven from Water

Crop Failures Increase

Crops Devastated

Cross-Breeding

Crumbling Roads, Buildings,
  and Sewage Systems

Cryptococcal Disease

Curriculum Change

Cyclones (Australia)

Damselflies Forced Back to UK

Danger to Kid's Health

Darfur

Dartford Warbler Plague

Daylight Increase

Deadly Virus Outbreaks

Death Rate Drop

Death Rate Increase (USA)

Deaths to Reach Six Million

Decades of Progress at Risk

Dengue Hemorrhagic Fever

Depression

Desert Advance

Desert Retreat

Destruction of the
  Environment

Dig Sites Threatened

Disasters

Diseases Move North

Diving Reefs Closed

Dog Disease

Dozen Deadly Diseases (or Not)

Drought

Ducks and Geese Decline

Dust Bowl in the Corn Belt

Dust Doubles

Earlier Pollen Season

Earth Axis Tilt

Earth Biodiversity Crisis

Earth Crumbling

Earth Dying

Earth Even Hotter

Earth to Explode

Earth on Fast Track

Earth Light Dimming

Earth Lopsided

Earth Melting

Earth Morbid Fever

Earth Past Point of No Return

Earth Slowing Down

Earth Spins Faster

Earth Upside Down

Earthquakes

Earthquakes Redux

El Niño Intensification

Emerging Infections

Encephalitis

End of the World as We Know It

English Villages Lost

Equality Threatened

Europe Simultaneously Baking and Freezing

Eutrophication

Everyplace Hit Hardest

Expansion of University Climate Groups

Experts Muzzled

Extinctions

Extreme Changes to California

Fading Fall Foliage

Famine

Farm Output Boost

Farmers Benefit

Farmers Go Under

Farming Soil Decline

Fashion Disaster

Fever

Figurehead Sacked

Fir Cone Bonanza

Fires Fanned in Nepal

Fish Bigger

Fish Catches Drop

Fish Deaf

Fish Downsize

Fish Feminized

Fish Get Lost

Fish Head North

Fish Lopsided

Fish Shrinking

Fish Stocks Decline

Fish Stocks at Risk

Five Million Illnesses

Flesh-Eating Disease

Flies on Everest

Flood of Migrants

Flood Patterns Change

Flood Preparation for Crisis

Floods

Floods of Beaches and Cities

Flora Dispersed

Florida Economic Decline

Flowers in Peril

Flowers Wilt

Flying Squirrels Move Up

Fog Decrease in San Francisco

Fog Increase in San Francisco

Food Poisoning

Food Prices Rise

Food Prices Soar

Food Production Increased

Food Safety Affected

Food Security Threat (SA)

Football Team Migration

Forest Decline

Foundations Increase Grants

Foundations Threatened

Frog with Extra Heads

Frost

Frost Damage Increased

Frostbite

Fungi Fruitful

Fungi Invasion

Fungi Rot the World

Games Change

Garden of Eden Wilts

Geese Decline in Hampshire

Gene Pools

Genetic Changes

Genetic Diversity Decline

Geysers Imperiled

Giant Icebergs (Arctic)

Giant Icebergs (Australia)

Giant Oysters Invade

Giant Pythons Invade

Giant Squid Migrate

Gingerbread Houses Collapse

Glacial Earthquakes

Glacial Retreat

Glacier Grows (California)

Glacier Wrapped

Glaciers on Snowden

Glass Melts

Global Cooling

Glowing Clouds

Golf Course to Drown

Golf Masters Wrecked

Grain Output Drop (China)

Grain Output Stagnating
   (India)

Grandstanding

Grasslands Wetter

Gravity Shift

Great Barrier Reef 95 Percent Dead

Great Tits Cope

Greening of the North

Grey Whales Lose Weight

Gulf Stream Failure

Hantavirus Pulmonary Syndrome

Harvest Increase

Harvest Shrinkage

Hay Fever Epidemic

Health Affected

Health of Children Harmed

Health Risks

Health Risks (Even More)

Heart Attacks and Strokes (Australia)

Heart Deaths

Heart Disease

Heat Waves

Hedgehogs Bald

Hibernation Affected

Hibernation Ends Too Late

Hibernation Ends Too Soon

Home Runs

Homeless Fifty Million

Hornets

Human Development Faces Unprecedented Reversal

Human Fertility Reduced

Human Health Risk

Human Race Oblivion

Human Rights Violations

Hurricane Reduction

Hurricanes

Hurricanes Fewer

Hurricanes More

Hurricanes Not

Hydropower Problems

Hyperthermia Deaths

Hypothermia Deaths

Ice Age

Ice Hockey Extinct

Ice Sheet Growth

Ice Sheet Shrinkage

Ice Sheet Tipping Point

Icebergs

Illegal Immigration

Illness and Death

Inclement Weather

India Drowning

Indigestion

Industry Threatened

Infectious Diseases

Inflation in China

Infrastructure Failure
(Canada)

Insect Explosion

Insect Invasion

Insurance Premium Rises

Inuit Displacement

Inuit Poisoned

Inuit Suing

Invasion of Alien Worms

Invasion of Antarctic Aliens

Invasion of Asian Carp

Invasion of Cane Toads

Invasion of Caterpillars

Invasion of Cats

Invasion of Crabgrass

Invasion of Herons

Invasion of Jellyfish

Invasion of King Crabs

Invasion of Lampreys

Invasion of Midges

Invasion of Pine Beetles

Invasion of Rats (China)

Invasion of Slugs

Island Disappears

Islands Sinking

Italy Robbed of Pasta

Itchier Poison Ivy

Japan's Cherry Blossom
Threatened

Jellyfish Explosion

Jets Fall from Sky

Kew Gardens Taxed

Kidney Stones

Killer Cornflakes

Killing Us

Kitten Boom

Koalas' Leaves Inedible

Koalas under Threat

Krill Decline

Lake Empties

Lake Shrinking and Growing

Landslides

Landslides of Ice at 140 MPH

Large Trees Decline

Lawsuit Successful

Lawsuits Increase

Lawyers' Income Increased
(Surprise, Surprise!)

Z

Mortality Lower

Mosquitoes Adapting

Mountain (Everest) Shrinking

Mountaineers Fears

Mountains Break Up

Mountains Green and
    Flowering

Mountains Taller

Mubarak Fall

Musk Ox Decline

Myanmar Cyclone

Narwhals at Risk

Narwhals Suffocate

National Parks Damaged

National Security Implications

Native Wildlife Overwhelmed

Natural Disasters Quadruple

Neurological Diseases

New Islands

Next Ice Age

NFL Threatened

Nile Delta Damaged

No Effect in India

Noctilucent Clouds

Northwest Passage Opened

Nuclear Plants Bloom

Oaks Dying

Oaks Move North

Obesity

Oblivion

Ocean Acidification

Ocean Acidification Faster

Ocean Dead Spots

Ocean Dead Zones Unleashed

Ocean Deserts Expand

Ocean Oxygen Crisis

Ocean Salt Extremes

Ocean Waves Speed Up

Olympic Games to End

Opera House to Be Destroyed

Outdoor Hockey Threatened

Owls Turn Brown

Oxygen Depletion Zones

Oyster Herpes

Ozone Repair Slowed

Ozone Rise

Peat Bogs No Problem

Peat Bogs Problem

Penguin Chicks Frozen

Penguin Chicks Smaller

Penguin Populations
    Devastated

Z

Rivers Raised

Road Accidents

Roads Wear Out

Robins Rampant

Rocky Peaks Crack Apart

Roof of the World a Desert

Rooftop Bars

Rose by Any Other Name
    Smells of Nothing, A

Ross River Disease

Russia under Pressure

Salinity Increase

Salinity Reduction

Salmon Stronger

Salmonella

Sardine Run Unpredictable

Satellites Accelerate

Schmallenberg Virus

School Closures

Sea Level Rise

Sea Level Rise Faster

Sea Snot

Seals Mating More

Seismic Activity

Severe Thunderstorms

Sewer Bills Rise

Sex Change

Sexual Dysfunction

Sexual Promiscuity

Shark Attacks

Sharks Booming

Sharks Hybridize

Sharks Moving North

Sheep Change Color

Sheep Shrink

Shop Closures

Short-Nosed Dogs Endangered

Shrimp Sex Problems

Shrinking Ponds

Shrinking Sheep

Shrinking Shrine

Ski Resorts Threatened

Skinks Impacted

Slavery

Slow Death

Smaller Brains

Smog

Snow Thicker

Snowfall Decrease

Snowfall Heavy

Snowfall Increase

Soaring Food Prices

Z

Societal Collapse

Soil Change

Soil Subsidence

Songbirds Change Eating
Habits

Sour Grapes

Soybean Crop to Drop

Space Junk Increase

Space Problem

Spectacular Orchids

Spider Bites to Increase

Spider Danger in UK

Spiders Getting Bigger

Spiders Invade Scotland

Squid Aggressive Giants

Squid Larger

Squid Population Explosion

Squid Tamed

Squirrels Reproduce Earlier

Starfish Sperm Eaten by
Parasites

Stingray Invasion

Storm Damage Costs Rise

Storms Wetter

Stratospheric Cooling

Street Crime to Increase

Subsidence

Suicide

Sunset Displaced

Swordfish in the Baltic

Sydney Opera House Wiped
Out

Tabasco Tragedy

Taxes

Tea Flavor Change

Tectonic Plate Movement

Teenage Prostitution

Terrorists (India)

Thatched Cottages at Risk

Threat to Peace

Ticks Move Northward
(Sweden)

Tides Rise

Tigers Drown

Tigers Eat People

Tomatoes Rot

Tornado Outbreak

Tourism Increase

Toxic Seaweed

Trade Barriers

Trade Winds Weakened

Traffic Jams

Transport Snarl

Transportation Threatened

Z

Z

PHOTO CREDITS

All photography and artwork used in the interior design of this book is courtesy of www.shutterstock.com with the exception of the Rajendra Pachauri image. Special photo credits are listed below:

Al Gore (page 4, 82): stocklight/Shutterstock.com

Osama bin Laden (page 19): Asianet-Pakistan/Shutterstock.com

Matt Damon (page 38): Featureflash/Shutterstock.com

City bus (page 40): Chris Jenner/Shutterstock.com

Leonardo DiCaprio (page 43): s_bukley/Shutterstock.com

Homer Simpson Stamp (page 56): Andy Lidstone/Shutterstock.com

Georgia Guidestones (page 74): SeanPavonePhoto/Shutterstock.com

Hitler Stamp (page 91): mrHanson/Shutterstock.com

Lisa Jackson (page 100): Joe Seer/Shutterstock.com

Al Gore (page 125): stocklight/Shutterstock.com

NASA (page 134): Edwin Verin/Shutterstock.com

Nobel Peace Prize stamp (page 138): catwalker/Shutterstock.com

Barack Obama (page 142): spirit of america/Shutterstock.com

Yoko Ono (page 147): s_bukley/Shutterstock.com

Rajendra Pachauri (page 152): Marshall Niles, Marshall Niles Photography 2013

George Soros (page 197): Adrin Shamsudin/Shutterstock.com

Margaret Thatcher (page 211): David Fowler/Shutterstock.com

Ted Turner (page 215): Helga Esteb/Shutterstock.com

United Nations (page 218): Songquan Deng/Shutterstock.com

Wikipedia (page 229): Annette Shaff/Shutterstock.com